It is an honor and joy to ____ spiritual daughter and po____ Mercy Lokulutu. Her bold passion, audacious faith, and utter obedience to God will inspire you. It will also challenge you in the best way. This book is her life message: to live a life of surrender to God. One of the greatest ways to express our love to God is to yield our lives to Him. It can be high-risk and high-cost, but in the process of surrender we learn more of who God is and who we are truly created to be. Read Mercy's book and start this journey today.

—STOVALL WEEMS
LEAD PASTOR, CELEBRATION CHURCH

Living an "as You wish" life, as portrayed by Mercy Lokulutu, will challenge you to draw closer to our Master, Jesus Christ, choose to obey Him, and to embrace the life design He has prepared for you. Mercy truly knows the joys of serving Him and shares from her life beautifully.

—JEAN OHLERKING
COFOUNDER AND VICE PRESIDENT,
CHILDREN'S CUP

As You Wish is not only Mercy's story of surrender and dying to herself but also a call for every Christ follower to experience what Jesus said in Matthew 16:25: "If you try to hang on to your life, you will lose it. But if you give up your life for my sake, you will save it" (NLT). Through personal stories and life experiences she shares how she came to the defining moment when she chose to say, "As You wish," and discovered her greatest fulfillment. Mercy's passion for Christ and seeing others experience the "as You wish" life are woven into each page. Her story will challenge and empower many to let go and experience freedom through surrender.

—DARRYL AND KARA BELLAR
LEAD PASTORS, THE JOURNEY CHURCH

AS YOU
WISH

AS YOU
WISH

MERCY LOKULUTU

PASSIO
THE ART OF AUTHENTIC FAITH

As You Wish by Mercy Lokulutu
Published by Passio
Charisma Media/Charisma House Book Group
600 Rinehart Road
Lake Mary, Florida 32746
www.charismahouse.com

Cover design by Lisa Rae Cox
Design Director: Bill Johnson

Visit the author's website at www.mercylokulutu.com.

Library of Congress Control Number: 2013911068
International Standard Book Number: 978-1-62136-255-5

E-book ISBN: 978-1-62136-256-2

While the author has made every effort to provide accurate telephone numbers and Internet addresses at the time of publication, neither the publisher nor the author assumes any responsibility for errors or for changes that occur after publication.

First edition

13 14 15 16 17 — 9 8 7 6 5 4 3 2 1
Printed in the United States of America

*With utmost love and honor, I dedicate
this book to my beloved mother,
Pauline Makka.*

*She lived a life worthy of her calling
and faithfully sowed seeds that will
reap eternal and everlasting fruit.*

CONTENTS

ACKNOWLEDGMENTS

FIRST AND FOREMOST I want to thank my family for tirelessly working with me on this book. To my beloved husband, Bosulu, who shows me love that knows no bounds, thank you for believing in me even when I didn't believe in myself. To Isaiah and Ava-Pauline, you are my greatest inspiration and give me hope for the future. God blessed me extravagantly, as life with you is beyond my wildest dreams! I am deeply grateful to my father, Fidelis Makka, and my sisters Blessing, Serah, and Faith, who are as much a part of this journey as I am. Thank you all for your incessant encouragement and belief that with God all things are possible. I could not have done this without you.

Part of the beauty of birthing a dream is that God brings midwives and co-laborers to share the pain and magnify the joy of seeing new life emerge. Much appreciation goes to my incredible church family at Celebration in Jacksonville, Florida. This book is as much a part of you as it is of me. Thank you for always believing in me. Despite distance or geography, we will always grow together because we share the same roots. I know the best is yet to come! To my church family at DC Metro Church in Alexandria, Virginia, thank you for embracing me with open arms. It's an honor to serve in God's house and build alongside all of you. To all who gave me advice, lent a listening ear, and offered generosity of heart, you have helped this dream become a reality, and your reward is in heaven!

To the dream team at Charisma House who provided invaluable assistance in editing and revising and then doing it all over again, I thank you for your wisdom and partnership.

A special tribute goes to Pastors Stovall and Kerri Weems. Words don't suffice to express my thanks, so the best gratitude I can offer is to courageously walk out my God-given destiny just as you've taught me. You will always be a part of my spiritual life in the most special way as my spiritual father and mother. Your willingness to pay the price of surrender inspires me.

Also, to all the great men and women of God who have been mentors for me and invested in my life, you are my heroes and heroines, and yours are the shoulders on which I humbly stand. Thank you for being trailblazers, for boldly paving the way, imparting vision, and challenging me to be all God created me to be. I pray I am able to do the same for those coming after me.

FOREWORD

L ET ME START by admitting that I am more than just a little bit biased about Mercy Lokulutu. We are not merely professional acquaintances; we are up-close, personal friends. I love her strength, her humor, and her contagious passion for the things of God. But the thing I love the most about her is her deep commitment to the message of this book. Mercy lived the words "as You wish," long before they ever found their way onto the pages of this book. But you will see for yourself that "as You wish" was not always her first response to the call and will of God.

From the time I first met Mercy, I could sense a special *something* about her. We jokingly referred to her as the Nigerian princess because of the regal manner in which she carried herself and the respect she naturally commands when she walks into a room, even before she utters a word. And yet, in those early days, for all her warm openness and leadership potential, I sensed she was still tentative, testing the waters but not yet ready to dive in to the deep.

As the years passed, it was a joy to see Mercy slowly begin to drop the veil of hesitancy and fully embrace the will of God for her life. She served faithfully in our church in nearly every area. The humility wrought through

her service wove together beautifully with her natural
nobility and dignity to create a garment of grace worthy
of a woman who was poised to be launched by God into a
greater purpose. Reading the pages of this book has given
me a look into the work the Holy Spirit was doing behind
the scenes during this time. What an honor and joy to
have played a small part in His work in her life!

There is nothing more rewarding for a pastor than
seeing those whom they have led and nourished in Christ
boldly fulfill their function in the body of Christ to their
best potential. I still remember the very first time Mercy
preached in church. Her message was entitled "As You
Wish." It was then that I saw in full force for the first time
the incredible gift of speaking that was upon Mercy's life.
My heart was so full that day, and I continue to be proud
of her as a daughter in Christ as she pursues Christ with
courageous faith.

More than just a good communicator, Mercy is an
anointed minister. She doesn't simply "preach a good
message," but the Lord also uses her to *impart* something
from heaven into the lives of those who hear her speak.
However, such a ministry is never born in the spotlight, but
in secret. It springs from deep and continued surrender in
times when no one seems to notice or even care that you
are saying to God, "Yes, Father, as You wish."

In a day when talented communicators abound, I believe
God is raising up a generation of ministers for whom
speaking and writing are simply vessels of impartation
to build His church. Mercy Lokulutu is undoubtedly a
woman of this generation.

I am confident that as you read this book you will learn,
as Mercy did, the utter beauty of surrender to God. You

will learn that true freedom is not doing as you wish, but saying to your ever-faithful heavenly Father, "Yes, Lord, as You wish."

—KERRI WEEMS
LEAD PASTOR, CELEBRATION CHURCH
JACKSONVILLE, FL

INTRODUCTION

I BELIEVE ALL OF us have a life message—a message that comes from the school of life with Jesus rather than an academic education, a message that lives and breathes in and through us, so much so that it writes itself. It's a message that goes beyond the pages of books into the cellular makeup of our spirits. It wills...no, *demands*...an expression in black words on white paper. This message is not derived from hours of studying but rather inspired in solitary moments—a whisper in the ear, a shifting of the heart, a change of posture and stance. It is the product of adversity, the fruit of seeds of suffering sown in tears and reaped with the sickle of faith. You don't have to preach this message because you *are* the message, your life so entrenched in Christ that you can no longer separate where one life ends and the other begins. What you are about to read is my life's message, and you are part of a supernatural transaction between me, you, and God. This message guides how your life continues to unfold; it instructs every action and outlook. It announces your arrival to the world.

The greatest commandment we have is to love God, and the nature of true love is to bring pleasure to the one who is loved. When Jesus prayed in the garden, He said, "Father, if it is possible, let this cup pass from Me, nevertheless, not my will, but Yours be done." (See Matthew 26:39; Luke 22:42.) What Jesus was really saying was, "Father, as You wish." This is true love. Jesus did not only speak about surrender; He also lived it. Jesus was willing to embrace the death of His body and His own desire, and He asks us to do the same. Let go of your plans for your life, release the dreams you've nurtured in your heart, liberate your aspirations. Love the Lord your God with reckless abandon—without reservation or personal agenda. This is surrender. It's living every day saying to God, "As You wish."

In our relentless pursuit of God, as we try to discover His purpose and destiny for our lives, we will struggle with letting go of our hopes and desires, both sacred and secular. We will stumble upon the Goliath of our selfish desires, our fleshly needs, and our own wisdom. Surrender is both the only rock that will topple the goliath of self and also what positions us in the slingshot of God's hands. He prepares us and, when we are willing, propels us into the world. We will want to hold tightly to what is safe and does not require total dependence on God. If we are not careful, the very comfort with which God has blessed us will become a distraction. We hesitate to put a knife to the throat of our dreams even when God asks us to. Because why would God allow you to dream, actually make those dreams come true, and then take it all away in an instant? We forget that the dream is not the prize; God is. It is in those times that we need to raise the white flag of our lives and truly surrender.

There is a certain place you will reach when you live for God. It is a place that tests your surrender and forces you to decide, once and for all, whether you trust the God you love. I have been there.

You will know when you have reached your own place. It is a state where your selfish dreams and God's plan for your life violently collide, and only one of the two will survive. It will test your love for God and your resolve to surrender to Him. No one will have to mark your place out for you because it will mark you deeply and permanently. When you reach that place, when you are praying and crying in the garden of your own Gethsemane and deciding whether to drink the cup of God's will for your life or to reject His will for one of your own making, I pray you have the strength to surrender and say, just as Jesus did, *"Father, as You wish."*

whose life am I living?

Chapter One

WHOSE LIFE IS IT ANYWAY?

"I've been saying it so long to you, you just wouldn't listen. Every time you said, 'Farm Boy, do this,' you thought I was answering, 'As you wish,' but that's only because you were hearing wrong. 'I love you' was what it was, but you never heard."[1]
—WILLIAM GOLDMAN

We are managers of God's estate.

YOUR LIFE IS not your own. Perhaps this comes as a huge surprise to you or no surprise at all, but either way it's absolutely true. I'm not sure how God speaks to you, but sometimes He uses some arbitrary ways to capture my heart.

The Princess Bride happens to be one of my favorite movies of all time. There is a particular line in that movie that grips my heart every time I hear it. In case you lived under a rock in the late nineties and missed the phenomenon that is *The Princess Bride*, you need to put this book down and run to the nearest movie store or Redbox kiosk to rent it! Just kidding, you don't have to go right this minute, but certainly in the near future. This movie has everything you need in a romantic comedy—scaling cliffs of insanity; battling rodents of unusual size; surviving a kidnapping by a trio of outlaws; and disrupting an impromptu, sham wedding—hey, all the ladies out there understand that true love doesn't come easy!

It's a classic fairy tale about Westley, an ordinary farmhand, who is in love with the beautiful and nymph-like Princess Buttercup. Though he knew his love was unrequited, every time Buttercup orders him to do something, even a menial task, Westley would always respond with only three words: *As you wish.*

The narrator then adds this profound thought: "[Princess Buttercup] was amazed to discover that when he was saying, *'As you wish,'* what he really meant was, *'I love you.'*"[2] Because of his love for Buttercup, Westley was willing to surrender his desires, his pride, and his will to her every whim. It was while watching this scene that I heard, as clear as day, the Holy Spirit whisper to my heart to read the story of Jesus in the Garden of Gethsemane.

I was amazed by both the clarity of His voice and the softness of the prompting. I would really love to tell you I am so spiritual that I immediately leapt to my feet and raced to read my Bible, but I didn't. I sat there for a few seconds thinking, "Is this really God, or did I just make up that voice in my head? The movie is just getting to the good swashbuckling part!" I am so glad I decided against that and stopped the movie, picked up my women's devotional Bible, and thumbed to the Book of Luke to read the story of Jesus in the Garden of Gethsemane.

Luke's account of this scene tells us that Jesus went up to the Mount of Olives, with His disciples, to pray before He would be handed over to the authorities to be crucified. Jesus was facing the ultimate test of His love as He was about to suffer the cruelest form of death imaginable. On His obedience, literally, *hung* the salvation of billions upon billions of lives. If He fails, no one gets saved; if He succeeds, the spiritual landscape of the world is forever changed. No pressure, right? Jesus was literally sweating blood in agony for what He was about to endure, and His response fully displays both His deity and His humanity. Luke 22:41–42 says, "He withdrew about a stone's throw beyond them [the disciples], knelt down and prayed, 'Father, if you are willing, take this cup from me; yet not my will, but yours be done.'" I am amazed by His surrender in this moment. It astounds me that of all the prayers Jesus could utter in that moment, the one that left His lips was, "Father, not My will, but Yours be done." Jesus was saying, "Father, as You wish." And ultimately, He was saying, "Father, I love You."

Eureka! Here was what I now saw revealed in this passage: love is the key to surrender, and because of His great love

[handwritten margin note: aren't I saying this?]

for His Father and the world, Jesus willingly surrendered His desires, His pride, and His will to God. This act of love was what gave Him the strength to overcome the cross, to conquer the grave, and to be seated at the right hand of God. I don't surrender to God because I have to or because it's the Christian thing to do or out of a sense of duty. I surrender because of love. Who knew such insightful revelation could be embedded in a movie with bad eighties' hair and what we thought were superb graphics?

Jim Elliot says it this way: "He is no fool who gives up what he cannot keep to gain what he cannot lose."[4] This is so true when it comes to surrendering to God. In spite of what the world tries to tell us, our lives are not our own. Burger King is wrong: you can't always have it your way. You will never find satisfaction doing life your way, following your own rules, and being a god unto yourself. God's way is always infinitely better than anything our minds can conjure up. If your life is truly not your own, you have nothing to lose by giving it to the One who created you.

Think about the differences between Adam and Jesus: both of them had a garden "moment" where one decided to go his own way in an act of deliberate, measured disobedience, and the other simply said, "As You wish." In the Garden of Gethsemane Jesus reclaimed all that Adam lost in the Garden of Eden. Adam took what did not belong to him—he became a thief—and was cast out of paradise. Jesus, on the other hand, turned *to* a thief, while on the cross and said, "Today you will be with *me* in paradise" (Luke 23:43, emphasis added). Adam was tested in a garden surrounded by beauty, love, and perfection. Jesus was tested in another type of garden: a crushing

4

olive press, surrounded by the silence of friends, sweating drops of blood and praying words of agony.

The Old Testament is a record of the lineage of Adam (Gen. 5:1), and it ends with a curse (Mal. 4:6). Jesus Christ ushers in a new pedigree, a new family tree carved with grace and mercy (Matt. 1:1), and His legacy ends like this in Revelation 22: "And there shall be no more curse" (v. 3, NKJV). Adam's path led to death, but Jesus's path leads to life everlasting. The first Adam took the fruit of life, but no one took the last Adam's life from Him. He freely laid it down.[4]

Giving someone else complete control of your life is counterintuitive to what the world tells us. The world is constantly telling us that we can help ourselves, and indeed the best-selling department in almost every bookstore is the "self-help" category of books. If we aren't careful, we can allow the world around us to dictate to us instead of us changing the culture we are in. Surrender is not a popular idea because it seems like the least likely path to discovering the truth of who we really are in Christ, but therein lies the paradox. A paradox is a statement that is actually true but, because it is contrary to conventional wisdom, it seems absurd.

Let's look at a few paradoxical ideas that at first may seem counterintuitive, but when we look at them through an eternal perspective, we see the wisdom of the Word of God.

1. Death brings life—the world says save your life; God says die to self (Gal. 2:20; John 12:24).

2. Receive through giving—the world says work, earn, and save all you can while you can. God says it's better to give than receive (Acts 20:35).

3. The last will be first—the world says strive to be the first even if it means putting yourself ahead of others. God says the best way to lead is to serve (Matt. 20:25–28).

4. We are in the world but not of the world— the world says it will satisfy all our needs (John 15:19); God says He will satisfy all our needs (Phil. 4:19).

5. Weakness is strength—the world says we should be proud of our strength and avoid suffering; God says take pleasure in suffering because when you're weak, He is strong in you (2 Cor. 12:10).

thank God

We have to reject what the world thinks about surrender and realize that surrender means you gain something, not lose everything. The truth is that what we have to gain from offering the totality of who we are to the very able hands of God is far greater than anything we can do with our lives by ourselves. As counterintuitive as it may seem, if you want to discover who you really are, you must first surrender to God. This kind of thinking makes no sense to the natural mind, which is why we have to employ more than just our minds if we are truly going to surrender to God. We are triune beings: body, soul, and spirit, made in the image of God.

Triune Living

Romans 12:1–2 provides a beautiful illustration of an "as You wish" lifestyle—body, soul, and spirit. Paul, like the well-versed lawyer that he is, dexterously argues a brilliant case for the need to live an "as You wish" life. Paul is a skillful maestro, directing his words like a well-rehearsed concert band with its cadence and measure perfectly placed.

First, Paul sets an urgent tempo by begging us in the strongest and most earnest of terms. He says this message needs immediate attention; you can't afford to wait! My professional training as a registered nurse allows me say with certainty that if someone came into an urgent care center with a broken leg, no prudent person would advise them to go home and see their primary physician in his office the next day. The broken leg needs immediate attention because the consequences of not taking care of it will be dire and possibly fatal. This is the same message Paul is trying to convey to us: don't put this off. Address whether you are living surrendered to God or not immediately because the cost of putting this off can be dire and even fatal spiritually.

> If you want to discover who you really are, you must first surrender to God.

Next, Paul says we should offer our bodies to God, but he doesn't stop there; he tells us to have the mercies of God in view as we do this. There is a reason Paul tells us to do this. He knows that it's hard, in our human thinking, to view surrender positively. So Paul is saying if you're having a hard time trusting God enough to surrender your life to

7

Him, then think about how good He's been to you, how He forgives your sins, heals your diseases, redeems your life from the pit, and crowns you with love and compassion. (See also Psalm 103:2–5.) When you struggle in the process of surrendering to God, think of how merciful God has been to you and all the blessings you have in your life. If nothing else, you can thank God that He woke you up to a new day. Thankfulness removes the restraint of selfishness in your life.

I remember when my son was young and would complain that he didn't have the latest toys. One day my then three-year-old, Isaiah, thumbed through a newspaper flyer advertising new toys and bitterly grumbled, "It's not fair! I can't believe I only have four Transformers." Now, I did everything to restrain myself from laying hands on the child (and I don't mean in the prayerful kind of way).

I got down to his level, looked him in the eyes, and told him that some children didn't have any toys or even food. His big brown eyes widened, and he softly said, "That makes me so sad. Maybe they can have some of my toys." By giving him some perspective on being thankful for what he had, my son was able to be less self-centered. I know the issues in your life are much more serious than toys; life can be very painful.

Perhaps God hasn't answered all your prayers, and at this point your life has not turned out the way you hoped. You can still be thankful by focusing on the mercies of God. If nothing else, you can be thankful that you still have life in you, and that while you're still alive, God has a plan for your life.

Paul continues the stanza by focusing on surrendering our bodies. In Hebrew culture your body symbolized more

8

than your physical body, it was a representation of your entire life. I think both concepts work together beautifully. God wants us to surrender our lives, including our physical bodies.

I am enamored with the fact that God cares about my physical body, so much so that He made me in His image. What a magnificent concept! The image of *knitting a child in a mother's womb* (Ps. 139:13) speaks to such tender love and attention to detail. If you've ever watched someone knit a blanket or a hat, you can't rush this job, it takes fastidious patience and attention to detail to knit anything.

If you are a parent, then you remember staring intently at the gray, hazy screen in an obstetrician's office, trying to discern the outline of what looked remotely like your unborn child. I recall lying on the table with bated breath as the sonographer covered my huge belly in gel and scanned slowly over the arched landscape of it to give me the very first glimpse of each of my children.

To see their forms, the light gray outline of a fetus, a round head, the bulging tummy, tiny fingers and toes, the curvature of the spine, and finally, the comforting, pulsating rhythm of a beating heart—oh, I will always remember the first time I heard that familiar two-beat cadence of my baby's heart. It brought such unspeakable joy that it literally took my breath away. It remains an indelible memory in my heart. The thought of Creator God, master architect of the universe, who created legions of stars and galaxies, also allowing me to partner in creating and forming a precious life. That would have been enough, but He then allows my womb to cradle and nourish that life to maturity—it's almost too much to fathom!

In fact, when Jesus went to the cross to purchase our

freedom, part of that covenant was with our bodies as well as our souls. Genesis 17:13 says, "My covenant in your flesh is to be an everlasting covenant." This is why the act of circumcision was made on the body to show an outward sign of an inward covenant. This is also the reason the entire body is submerged beneath the water in baptism, just as Jesus's physical body was submerged.

Most astounding of all is the fact that our physical bodies house the same spirit of God that was once housed in the holy of holies. The presence of God that was once reserved to a most holy place only accessible by the high priest once a year is now fully available to everyone who accepts Jesus as Lord and Savior. Do you ever read the Bible and just marvel at the goodness of God? This is one of those realities that just leaves me slack-jawed and amazed—the spirit of the living God inside of me! What a phenomenal show of grace and love for God to entrust our human body to house our eternal spirit. How much more evidence do we need that God cares about our physical bodies? Our surrender to God has just as much to do with our bodies as anything else.

It's easy to hide our unsurrendered hearts because nobody can see inside of us, but it's harder to hide our unsurrendered bodies because everyone can see them. We are wearing the effects of our decisions. This is not to bring condemnation if you are struggling with weight issues or cutting your body or any other external vice; it is to encourage you that God actually cares about your physical body. He died so that we would not only be healed, but also so we would be whole.

Our whole body matters to God—body, soul, and spirit— and we all have a choice to make when it comes to those parts. The bottom line is this: either we surrender our body to God or to sin. Surrendering to one will feed contempt for the other. It's one or the other, not either/or and not both/and. Romans 6:12–13 says, "Therefore do not let sin reign in your mortal body, that you should obey it in its lusts. And do not present your members as instruments of unrighteousness to sin, but present yourselves to God as being alive from the dead, and your members as instruments of righteousness to God" (NKJV). The question is not if we are presenting our members as instruments but rather to whom? There are only two possible answers to that question, either sin or God. We must make a choice, and our actions speak louder than our words. Offer your body (your life) as though it were a sacrifice. The truth is, your refusal to surrender will be expressed in and through your body. It's not just your heart that can rebel against God; your physical body can too. Right now, you are either presenting your body to God in surrender or to sin in disobedience. Perhaps you need to make a decision right now to put some practical steps in place to surrender your body to God; perhaps it's a health decision or maybe it's saying no to sexual sin. No matter what the problem is, the solution is the same: Jesus. Make that decision right now and commit yourself to doing it by the grace of God.

JUMP IN THE BASKET

Paul ushers in a new measure with the idea of a living sacrifice. The concept of sacrificing something that yet lives is difficult to comprehend. What exactly does this look like? I once heard a poignant story that perfectly illustrates this idea. Have you ever heard a story that is so inspiring and challenging that it affects the way you view life? This is one of those stories for me, and the setting is a Sunday service in a small, remote African village. It was a familiar time in the service for this group of African Christians—the offering. Living in an agrarian culture, they bartered with goods, produce, and livestock rather than money. Each Sunday the offering was collected in large woven baskets, standing several feet tall in order to hold the live chickens, stalks of corn, bunches of bananas, and other goods that would be offered.

On this Sunday a particular little boy realized it was time for the offering and that he was empty-handed. He wanted to give God something, but he had nothing to give. Suddenly, he had an inspired thought, and as the big basket came by, he jumped in! "I'm giving *myself* to God," he audaciously announced. This story always makes my eyes brim with tears, as this young boy's simple faith astounds and challenges me. It causes me to understand more fully why Jesus exhorted us all to become like little children and humble ourselves as they do (Matt. 18:3–4).

I consider how much we struggle to give just 10 percent of our money in tithing, and we may think that is too much. The truth is, God doesn't just want 10 percent of your money; He wants *all* of your heart. In His omniscience He knows that where your money is, He will also find your heart. God did not surrender part of Jesus to save you. He gave Him up completely so that we could all be radically saved.

Why do we struggle so much to be living sacrifices for a God who sacrificed His best for us? Mostly because we are selfish by nature, we want to hold on to what we have and get more of it. From our toddler years when we learned what "mine" meant, we all relish the feeling of possessing things. If we continue down the path of always needing to possess things, those things eventually start to possess us. A. W. Tozer says:

> The blessed ones who possess the kingdom are they who have repudiated every external thing and have rooted from their hearts all sense of possessing. These are the poor in spirit.... These blessed poor are no longer slaves to the tyranny of things. They have broken the yoke of the oppressor; and this they have done not by fighting but by surrendering. Though free from all sense of possessing, they yet possess all things.[5]

Complete surrender to God will cost us something. The question remains: Are we willing to bear that cost? King David was a man after God's heart, and he said he would not sacrifice anything to God that did not cost him something (2 Sam. 24:24). Surrender costs us our self-centered nature; it costs us our selfish ambition. We cannot exalt God and ourselves at the same time. Many times our biggest distraction and obstacle in surrender is ourselves. The greatest enemy to surrender is self and selfish desires. It's not enough to deny yourself and surrender to God once, when you initially asked Jesus to come into your heart and to be your Savior. You must continue to surrender every day.

Continual, daily surrender is what will protect you from being the kind of living sacrifice that keeps crawling off the altar. We climb in the basket and crawl back out. I put my life on the altar and then crawl off and go do my own thing for a while. Have you ever done that? Have you ever made a decision to do something like pray daily, read your

Bible more, or give up a bad habit only to find yourself back in your old patterns? We all have. I wonder where you are right now. If you did an honest inventory, could you say that your life is on the altar of surrender, that you are fully surrendered to God, or have you crawled off somewhere? Surrender to God isn't something we just do once. It's a daily decision.

The progression in Paul's concerto reaches a final crescendo with a dramatic sequence: surrender is not only holy and acceptable but actually an act of worship! Some versions say a "spiritual act of worship." I know that can sound like Christian jargon or "Christianese," but the whole point of this passage is that our surrender to God should be deliberate and voluntary. In the Old Testament the act of worship was to sacrifice an animal, but in the New Testament we don't worship by taking the life of anyone else but rather by laying ours down. Frederick Bruce says, "The sacrifices of the new order do not consist in taking the lives of others, like the ancient animal sacrifices, but in giving one's own."[6]

> The greatest enemy to surrender is self and selfish desires.

The word *spiritual* in the Greek is *logikos*; we get the word *logical* from it. It can also be translated "reasonable."[7] Using that meaning, offering ourselves to God makes sense. Total surrender is the only rational course to take when you really see who God is and what He's done. Nothing else makes any sense. Halfway surrender is irrational. To decide to give part of your life to God and keep other parts for yourself—to say, "Everything is Yours, Lord, except for this relationship... except for this part of my heart... except for my money, except for my hidden sin..."—is irrational!

I don't know about you, but *worship* is not the first word that pops into my mind when I think of surrender. Some of the lies we have believed about what surrender means and what it looks like are just that, lies! Surrender does *not* mean you are a weakling, a doormat, or a loser. What it *does* mean is that you cease resisting to a power greater than you and make a deliberate decision to submit to that authority. To take it even a little deeper, God says when you do stop resisting Him and surrender, it looks like... worship!

Stop resisting God + Submit to God's authority = worship

Does it now make more sense as to why we raise our hands in worship? Raising your hands is a sign of surrender, a universal sign to any governing authority that says, "I will not resist any longer and I willingly submit myself to you." Surrender, as an act of worship, may be a foreign concept to you because you always associate worship with music. Worship is not a synonym for music. In the Bible worship predates music; Adam worshipped in the Garden of Eden, but no mention of music is made until Genesis 4:21.

Worship is not for your benefit; it is all about bringing pleasure to God. If you have ever gone to church and said, "I didn't 'get' anything out of the worship today," perhaps you worshipped for the wrong reasons. It's not about you; it's for God. Worship is not just so we can sing songs and mouth words. Beyond what we say, worship is who we are. God actually inhabits our worship. He does not just want us to go through the motions, He wants us to mean what we say and say what we mean. "These people come near to me with their mouth and honor me with their lips, but their hearts are far from me. Their worship of me is made up only of rules taught by men" (Isa. 29:13).

God does not accept anything offered to Him that is half-hearted and hypocritical. Selfish prayers, insincere praise, empty words, and man-made rituals with no meaning do not touch God's heart. He is not touched only by what we say; He is also touched by our heart and how we are living out what we're saying. The secret to a lifestyle of true worship is doing everything as if you were doing it for Jesus. Work becomes worship when you dedicate it to God and perform it with an awareness of His presence.

Sometimes we misunderstand what it means to be spiritual. Growing up, I thought being spiritual meant you had to be at church all the time, read your Bible most of the day, and have a holy "look," which was mostly quiet and serious. Based on that description, spiritual people did not look like they were having much fun. If they were happy, their faces surely did not show it, and I did not

Surrender to God isn't something we just do once. It's a daily decision.

want any part of that! Maybe you have the same false impressions that I had. Thankfully this is not an accurate perception of true spirituality.

In Scripture nobody is ever said to be filled with the Spirit unless you can see something in their behavior that gives outward evidence of the inward working in their lives. "Worship in spirit" is worship that others can see in us—consistent worship, active worship, joy-filled and enthusiastic worship. Worship should make a difference in how we handle our problems and relate to others; it should generate something in us that makes us act differently at work or at school. Worship should dramatically change our lives with evidence in our character and actions. Don't just display emotions on Sunday in church; also act with kindness and love on Monday through Saturday, because that is true worship.

You are made in the image of God, so when you receive Jesus, you have the Holy Spirit inside of you. You have been designed to communicate with Him. Worship is your spirit responding to God's Spirit. True worship is worship that is a natural by-product of a life that is surrendered to Christ that attracts those around us who are without Christ. We should not be so "spiritual" and "religious" that we cease to be relevant to the world around us, yet neither should we be so like the world that we don't stand out. An "as You wish" lifestyle is not partial or lopsided. It involves all of our beings—mind, body, and spirit. Romans 12:1–2 should be a guideline for every Christian; verse 1 tells us how to surrender, and verse 2 shows us how to stay surrendered to God.

Many of us start out sincerely chasing after God, but somewhere along the way we get distracted and lose our way. For some of us it's a trial or disappointment along the way that makes us reject the idea of surrendering to God because He let us down, and we don't trust Him. We have to reach a point where even though we don't understand God's ways, we can still trust His heart. If we allow the pain of life and the bitterness of suffering to take root in our hearts, before long we are off the path God has laid out for us. It is not enough to surrender to God once, when you initially asked Jesus to come into your heart and to be your Savior. You must continue to surrender day by day, decision by decision, minute by passing minute. I can say this with certainty because little did I know as I watched the movie that day, God was preparing my heart for my own garden scene and my own place of testing.

Chapter Two

A BATTLE OF WILLS

The more we let God take us over, the more truly our-
selves we become, because He made us.[1]
—C. S. LEWIS

I AM A DAUGHTER of Nigerian soil. My homeland is a country of vast beauty and rugged strength. Scenes dance across my mind—sitting under a blooming jacaranda sloppily eating mangoes, going shopping in the open air market with my mother, walking to school in an army green and white pinafore chatting with friends. My identity is framed and its edges sealed by the fact that I am African.

However, growing up I sensed that there were some disadvantages to being a woman. I always wondered why oftentimes a woman's identity was framed and structured by the men in her life. For example, women are sometimes introduced as the "daughter of so-and-so" or the "wife of so-and-so." This was especially true when you were in a situation where you needed to prove your authority. Sometimes people would even introduce a woman as the "mother of so-and-so" and name her son. Part of this is because of the culture of respect and honor in Nigeria that places great value on paternity, for which I am grateful.

On one hand there are aspects of my culture that I love and appreciate and will pass on to my children. There was another side of me, though, that pondered why we do things a certain way. My attitude as a young girl was one of inquisitive curiosity.

I would have quite a few questions when I heard someone say something such as, "Leave it for the women and the children." I would think, "Why are women grouped with children?" I wondered why some men had more than one wife but most women only had one husband. It baffled me to hear of a spouse's infidelity and for it to be explained away with a cliché phrase such as, "Oh, well, you know how men are!" I didn't know how men were, and I didn't understand the inconsistencies in how people treated men and women. It would have been easy, and even understandable, to develop a warped perception of womanhood. This would be the expected outcome unless you were raised by a woman who was secure in her identity, proud of her femininity, and courageous in her spirit. Luckily for me, I was raised by such an African woman.

My mother, Pauline Makka, was the kind of woman who was not bound by the chains of conformity. She did not get the memo about being a second-class citizen and forgot to remember that she was "just" a woman. She was the kind of woman who would show up at the men's prayer breakfast and challenge the men in the room to reevaluate their preconceived notions of gender roles. "When the Bible refers to men," my mother told them, "it says *mankind*. And *mankind* is inclusive of all genders, and therefore it is inclusive of *me*, a woman." Not only did she stay, but she also became the most faithful attendee of the "mankind prayer breakfast"—she eventually started hosting the breakfast meetings at our house!

As a child, I remember waking up at three o'clock in the morning and hearing her praying over me in tongues—I would just turn my pillow to the cool side, roll over, and go back to sleep because this was normal. I actually just assumed that all mothers, and certainly all Christian mothers, did this—get up even before the first cock crowed and pray over their children in tongues. It wasn't until I got older that I realized it wasn't normal and that she was way ahead of the times she happened to be born in. Trying to dissuade my mother from doing something she purposed to do was pointless. If it was in her heart to do, she was going to do it.

Sensing the call of God, she went into ministry in her thirties and became an ordained minister, a passionate evangelist, and a member of the Foursquare church board. She raised five children while maintaining a business, engaging in social justice causes, and bearing the burdens of life with wisdom, courage, and grace. She was not perfect by any means, but she led an extraordinary life. Simply put, I saw Jesus in my mother. Her attitude of surrender is deeply seared into my soul, and this greatly influences how I love my husband, how I raise my children, and how I serve God and people.

You should know that my mother was a first-generation Christian who was radically saved after an encounter with Jesus. People often ask me about the origin of my name, and she named me Mercy because she gave her life to Jesus while she was pregnant with me. Not only that, she changed the names of my two older sisters and gave them names that were reflective of her newfound faith in Jesus, Blessing and Serah. My younger sister, Faith, and my baby brother, Micah, joined our family later on. You should also know that she is my hero and the greatest influence in my spiritual life. My mother did not need to preach to her children about what it meant to be a follower of Jesus Christ. Words were hardly necessary because *she simply lived it.*

The fact that I am a woman does not make me a different kind of Christian, but the fact that I am a Christian does make me a different kind of woman.

She had a way about her—a heart of compassion to love the unlovable, to reach the despised, and to use her voice to bring freedom. I remember every Christmas Day wondering why our family was not gathering around a tree exchanging gifts like other families. We would attend church, share a big meal, and then cook huge pots of food that we would take out into the streets to the homeless and destitute. I also remember resenting this until I got older and realized the real gift of Christmas is Jesus, not the presents. It wasn't until I had firmly planted my feet in adulthood that I realized my mother was living with eternal perspective and kingdom purpose, and Christmas Day was no exception. Imagine that, a Christian actually being Christlike on, of all days, the day we celebrate the birth of Jesus!

My mother lived out the illustrious words of Elisabeth Elliot: "The fact that I am a woman does not make me a different kind of Christian, but the fact that I am a Christian does make me a different kind of woman."[2] She prayed incessantly, unceasingly, and tirelessly. I remember stealing glances at her face during our evening devotions, which sometimes were hours long. I knew I was supposed to be deep in prayer or enveloped in worship, but as a child I had the attention span of a hummingbird, so I always ended up people-watching instead. (Don't judge me!) I would glance sideways and see her out of the corner of my eye, tears streaming freely down her face as she sang love songs to her Savior, and I would wonder why she was crying. I would later find out the road that brought her to God had many twists and turns, and she truly understood how great a salvation God had gifted her with. Those who have been forgiven much, love much.

On many occasions my mom would gather her children at her feet and share her wisdom—everything from what kind of man to marry, to what kind of deodorant to wear, to how funny the last episode of *Tales by Moonlight*, an entertaining miniseries of children's folk tales, was. We would excitedly talk about the latest episode and what next week's show might hold for us. She was never too lofty to get down to our level, but we knew better than to have anything but the utmost respect for her. She definitely had that mom "look"—you know, the one that warns you that trouble is in your immediate future if you don't start behaving. Both she and my father inspired, rather than demanded, respect from their children.

My father is a brilliant, statuesque man; charismatic and articulate. I like to think I got my love for reading books and saving money from my dad, because he surely set an excellent example for both of those things! He has an affinity for research, is an avid reader, and always put a premium on academic excellence. My father served in the Nigerian military, and I remember seeing him in his full army uniform and feeling so proud to have a father who bounced his daughters on his knee in one moment and then bravely led platoons of soldiers out to war in another.

My parents sacrificed dearly to provide for their family, many times denying themselves so we could have what we needed. Words can't express how grateful I am that my parents had the foresight and wisdom to send us to a Christian school where we received a biblically sound and academically rigorous education. Hillcrest School is nestled in the picturesque city of Jos, where you will find gorgeous gentle, sloping hills, volcanoes, waterfalls, and vast basaltic plateaus. Hillcrest was beautiful not only because of the magnificent scenery but also because of the diversity of people. The student and teacher population was a melting pot of different countries and ethnicities. We certainly received a valuable education, but more than that we also developed rich relationships with people from diverse cultural backgrounds. This school built upon the rich spiritual foundation that my mother laid in our home, a structure that was as deep as it was high, and I am truly grateful for such a lasting, priceless investment into my life. As a pastor and preacher, she was anointed and commissioned by the Holy Spirit. She did not use her gender as an excuse to avoid fulfilling the purpose of God in her life. I will always admire my mother for the way she willingly used her gifts to serve her world. God blessed my mother with many gifts, one being encouragement and another being spiritual wisdom. When she preached and taught the Bible, she wielded her words with conviction and power. She would weave in real-life examples and illustrations like a masterful craftsman and incorporate hard-hitting truths from the Bible simultaneously. Her sermon jokes were actually funny, and she had a way of praying that let everyone in the room knew that she operated in an authority that does not come from title or position but rather from intimacy with God.

She loved the house of God, loved serving others, and lived to be in the presence of God. I remember watching her tithe faithfully whether we had little or much. There were times when we struggled financially, but her giving did not wane. In Nigerian culture, when people come to visit a family, they often give the children of the house gifts or sometimes even money. Anytime we would be given money, my mother would encourage us to tithe, planting seeds of faithful tithing and giving from an early age. The prosperous times did not distract her, and the lean times did not undo her. Words fail me as I try to capture an accurate picture of what an incredible woman of God my mother was. She was not perfect by any means, but I never doubted her love for her family, her country, and her God.

Darkness Within

I can't remember the exact moment I realized my mother was sick, but by the time I had moved away from home to attend college in the United States, I was fully aware. As a nineteen-year-old college student I had enough knowledge to understand what disease process she suffered from. She had developed high blood pressure in the course of having children, and it had started to affect her kidney function. Even from our weekly phone conversations, I could tell that she was not quite herself. My mom had a lively personality; it was easy to make her laugh, and she was always talkative, but lately she started sounding more tired.

I recall a conversation we had as I was deciding on what major to study, as many college freshmen do. I went back and forth between two different majors over and over again, making exhaustive lists of the pros and cons of each one. I excelled in the sciences; not many people can say they love microbiology lab, but I truly did. I was fascinated by the intricate and highly sophisticated cellular makeup of the human body, and many times I would wonder, "How can anyone be a scientist and not believe in God?" Science, for me, is like unwrapping an amazing gift from God, beholding something miraculous as each layer unfolds. I was drawn to health care and truly had a passion for working closely with people, so I thought the obvious path should be medical school.

However, there was something about the art and

science of nursing that drew me to that profession as well. I discussed the difficulty of this major life decision with my mother, and she challenged me to pray about it. She encouraged me to follow my passion and to know that no matter which path I took, God would use me for His glory. We prayed together, and over the course of a few weeks I made the decision to pursue a career in nursing.

You can start to understand now why I just *knew* God would heal even though her kidney function began to decline to the point where she needed dialysis, a procedure where a machine cleans and purifies your blood. This is the normal function of healthy kidneys, but her high blood pressure had damaged her kidneys so they did not function properly. As a family we rallied around her, we prayed for her healing, and we believed she would be healed. That is the simple truth. We just believed that God would heal her. The formula seemed pretty straightforward to me. "I know God heals" plus "I know my mother loves God" equals "God is going to heal my mother." Sometimes with God, however, the math does not add up. She didn't get better. She actually got worse, and it was determined that she needed a kidney transplant.

Being in nursing school, I understood the implications of what this disease was doing to my mother's body. Being her daughter, I reconciled something in my heart, that if it were possible, I would give the woman who gave *me* life a chance at life herself—one of my own kidneys. You only need one kidney, after all. We began the process of making plans for testing to see who was a match and who could donate a kidney. The donor process is quite lengthy, so there were many family discussions about the details. I do recall my father mentioning that India would be the preferred venue for the procedure because of their highly proficient doctors and advanced medical technology.

In the wake of this process my older sister and I decided to spend the summer at home with our family. My father picked us up from the airport in his tan-colored Toyota Land Cruiser, and we chatted and laughed all the way home. My mother met us at the door—she looked tired but hugged us with giddy excitement. I remember her hair was braided into cornrows, and entwined in each braid was more gray hair than I remembered. She had prepared my favorite dish, beans cooked in palm oil and sweet fried plantains—a meal that is both savory and sweet. That summer we went about our usual routines: family meals, church, laid-back evening walks.

One particular night, however, things seemed different. My mom had a particularly taxing day and was having a hard time getting comfortable enough to sleep that night. She kept moving from lying on the bed propped up by pillows to sitting upright in the chair. She didn't say too much, just asked for another pillow or a sip of water once in a while. Her condition worsened throughout the night and by the early morning hours she was having trouble breathing. My eldest sister, Blessing, a physician, understood the urgency of the situation, and my mom was quickly rushed to a nearby clinic.

It was clear that my mother needed emergent dialysis to remove all the extra fluid in her body that was making it difficult for her heart to expand fully and for full inspiration of air into her lungs. My dad also went to the hospital to be with her while I stayed at home with my younger siblings, Faith and Micah. Eventually I made it to the hospital, and although I kept asking how she was, the replies I received from everyone were terse and brief. We paced the waiting room while the medical staff assessed her in the triage room. Suddenly the people taking care of my mother started moving faster, and their words took on a different tone, more hushed but yet more urgent.

The sensory memory is an amazing thing as the details about the next few hours have affixed themselves in my mind like words carved deeply in stone. No matter how much time passes, that day stays with me like a scar; all I have to do is pick at it again to recall the emotions and exactly how I felt. I can remember minute details that, on an ordinary day, I would never even notice. But this was no ordinary day. The attendants rushed my mother to another room adjacent to the one she had previously been in. This room was hot and bare, with beige walls of an uneven texture and stained with some kind of brown liquid. There was a small window to the left of the room with a few glass panes missing. I remember how it smelled, like a concoction of rubbing alcohol and iodine. I think I will always remember that, because if I close my eyes right now, I am back in that hot room. The standing fan in the corner had layers of dust on each of its three blades, and I wondered why no one had turned it on, seeing how hot it was in that little room.

The stretcher with the two squeaky wheels was tilted at an odd angle. The nurses and aides circled around it, while someone yelled for oxygen, someone else ran up a staircase, and there was chaos all around. I remember praying, "God, You can't let this happen. She loves You, she serves You, and she's Your daughter. P-l-e-a-s-e calm this chaos." Even now it feels as though that day was a dream. I remember feeling numb that day—such an odd feeling, numbness. I would have expected to feel the active feelings of panic, anxiety, or fear, but numbness? I was frozen as I watched my beloved mother take her last breath.

As the chaos ensued, there I stood, a twenty-year-old me staring in disbelief at the lifeless body of the woman who had given me life and given so much of her life to others. The eyes that had looked upon the world with such great love were now shut, and it was beyond anyone's control. That mouth that had uttered the most powerful prayers I have ever heard lay still…silent. And those strong hands that had guided and comforted so many moved no more; they just lay there peacefully. Though I already knew why, I wondered why the sense of urgency was gone. I still wanted the medical team to be rushing around. I wanted them to still try to save her, to still *try* to resuscitate my mom. They couldn't just stop. They had to keep trying.

One of the doctors slowly guided us out of the room and told my father that my mother was dead. To hear someone actually say the word *dead* jarred me. How could he say that word with such ease? As the words left his mouth, I was shocked out of the state of numbness I was in and unspeakable terror gripped my heart. It felt like the sinking, nauseating feeling of a roller coaster that just keeps plummeting without the relief of knowing that the ride would eventually come to an end.

I dropped to my knees and wept, every fiber of my being willing her lungs and cells to expand, her veins to fill with life-giving, oxygenated blood, and her fingers to twitch, to move, anything. "My God, my God! Is this really how this is going to end? This can't be happening. Is it a dream? Please, God, let this be a nightmare, and wake me up right now!" We left the hospital in stunned silence and endured a ride home that seemed longer than it should have been. It was so unnatural not to have her in the car with us, just the beginning of a nightmarish experience.

That night our house was full of activity—family and friends came to offer their condolences, and I tried my best to avoid everyone. Quite frankly, no matter how sincere their attempts to comfort and encourage me, the intrusion of their presence only made things worse. I have learned that sometimes silence is more comforting than words could ever be. I sobbed quietly through most of that night, snapshots of the day popping into my head. I could not sleep because my mind would not let me rest; it kept forcing me to relive the graphic details of the horror of that day.

I woke up the next morning wanting desperately to drink some "milk of amnesia" and make it all go away, but it was still all too real. Was she really gone? Did my mother really die? The beacon of light in my life had been extinguished like the empty stillness of a wick being blown out. I felt empty. It was a negative space, like the void of light that is left when a candle goes out and darkness envelops it. Going into her room proved to be too painful. I crumpled into a heap as I crossed the threshold of the door. Oh, just to hear her voice...but all I heard was silence, pregnant and weighty. In the emptiness of the days that followed, I endured the drudgery of details that accompany a death and tried to hold on for dear life. My heart was crushed; pain and disappointment were the mortar and pestle used. I raged against God in my heart.

DEEPER STILL

For the next few months I went back and forth through the stages of grief and added more stages of my own— bitterness, betrayal, and unforgiveness, to name a few. Little did I know, the family of grief had cousins and distant relatives who can hijack your journey to healing and set you back, if you're not careful. As if that was not devastating enough, just three years later I lost my fourteen-year-old brother, Micah, to sickle cell disease. I truly felt like the worst things that could ever happen to me in my life already did and there was nothing left to live for.

I found myself repeating the same prayers and reliving the same feelings. Honestly, at this point I wasn't even sure God loved me. I really didn't feel like His daughter. I would never treat anyone I loved the way I felt God was treating me. Feelings are not to be trusted when your heart is raw and grieving. "My God (I knew He was my Father, but I truly did not feel like a daughter), my God, are You really going to make me relive this terror again?" I think in that moment I finally understood, in part, how Jesus felt when He cried out, "My God, My God!" Even though He was the Son of God, at that moment on the cross Jesus felt separated from His Father, the gulf widened by the suffering He felt.

I doubted the sincerity of God's love for me. I wallowed in self-pity and retreated into a shell of a person. I vividly recall days when I wasn't sure whether I had taken a shower or not, and I think we can all agree that this is not a good place to be. (Let's face it, personal hygiene should just never be optional.) I was offended by God, at how He could heal other people in an instant but chose not to heal two people I loved so much. I just could not understand how God could allow them to die and inflict this kind of suffering on those He supposedly loved.

The onslaught of back-to-back tragedies was brutal to my tender heart. A portion of an entry in my journal from July 27, 2001, reveals my angst:

> Why do some people get healed and others die? In the uncertainty of life, the certainty of death puzzles and baffles me. Fear and doubt cackle and scoff at me, like annoying bugs that simply won't go away. I read something today that is so preposterous I actually laughed out loud when I read it. Spurgeon said, "I have learned to kiss the wave which cast me against the rock of ages." How is this possible? I know God is good, but nothing feels good right now.

My rebel heart reared its ugly head, and I actually had thoughts such as, "If God is good, then how could He do this? I'll never let my heart be hurt like this again. If this is what I get for being a Christian, then I don't think I want this." There were times I felt like God "owed me one" (it's a wonder that a bolt from heaven did not strike me down). I felt like I deserved to be angry, to feel betrayed, and to be bitter. I was consumed with thoughts that were deeply rooted in fear, unforgiveness, and bitterness. I had a hard time trusting God and others. I was miserable.

CALL TO DESTINY

One of Solomon's wise sayings in Proverbs 22:6 tells us: "Train up a child in the way he should go; even when he

33

is old he will not depart from it" (ESV). I know this is a true statement, but oh, did I try to turn away from the way I knew I should be going. I was never fully at peace with myself and was certainly not happy. I would try to go out partying with my friends and end up going home early and sitting on my couch with Ben and Jerry—not two guys...the ice cream. Even though I had made a conscious effort to turn my back on what I knew to be truth, I never felt completely at peace. However, even though I tried to run away from truth, the truth never departed from me.

I pray this comforts parents reading this that if you do your part to train up your child in the way they should go, even when they try to depart from it, it will never depart from them.

There were many adverse things I chose not to do, even in the gravity of my rebellion, simply because I had a relentless and persistent gnawing in my heart that urged me to fear God. As much as I wanted to, there was only so far I was willing to plummet into sin. It felt like there was an invisible line in my conscience that would allow me reach a certain point and no further. I now know that it was the protective hand of God, guiding me, even in my rebellion. Such a powerful picture of God's grace; unearned, undeserved, and unmerited but freely given as a gift.

As the months gradually turned into years, I grew increasingly uncomfortable with my life. It was a nagging feeling that refused to go away no matter how happy I tried to make myself. That feeling that I was missing something just would not go away. I wanted to feel complete, but I didn't. I wanted to feel truly happy, but I didn't. It seemed the more I tried to fill my life with activities, the emptier I felt.

I didn't have a dramatic transformation or a sudden out-of-this-world experience. For me it simply happened slowly over time. I reached a point where I realized that I am not smart enough to figure God out, *and that's OK*. What a novel thought, right? I came to peace with the fact that even though I didn't understand His ways, and never will, I still wanted to trust His love and His heart.

I wrestled with the idea of giving myself to God again, making myself vulnerable again. Somehow I knew this time it would be different. This time I wouldn't have my mother's coattail to ride on or her faith to hide behind. It was so easy to be a Christian when things were simple and life was easy. This was the first real test of my faith, and I sensed a point of no return in my relationship with God. I was struggling with the choice of whether to completely surrender myself to God or not.

> It's either all of Jesus or none at all. There is no such thing as halfway surrender.

I only had two choices: either I would trust Him with *all* of my heart or not at all. I learned the lesson that when it comes to surrender, there is no middle ground. You are forced to come to terms with who is in control of your life, and it's just not acceptable to "agree to disagree" with God about the direction your life should take. It's either all of Jesus or none at all. There is no such thing as halfway surrender.

ORDINARY YET SUPERNATURAL

On a warm Florida night three years after the ill-fated night I lost my mother, we had a women's gathering at church, and I tried to make excuses as to why I could not

35

go. However, my then-boyfriend, now-husband, convinced me to attend. I am eternally grateful for his persistence, although it annoyed me a bit at the time.

Looking back, it was such a mundane, ordinary moment, but it proved to be a defining moment of the highest proportion. So many times we zero in on the big, major events in our lives when in fact, your life can be supernaturally and completely altered by an ordinary decision. By simply saying yes to the right thing or no to the wrong thing, you can change your life forever.

I reluctantly went to church that night, not caring enough to even take my Bible with me. As I sat listening to the engaging minister, something began to happen in my heart. I didn't go to the altar or even raise my hand in response to the message. The best way I can describe it is that where there was once resistance to God in my heart, there no longer was. I had been thinking about my relationship with God and how off target I had drifted, and something gave way that night. It was as if there had been water shoring up behind a rock that had now broken through. It was a breakthrough. It was like an opening of my spiritual stance, a realization that I was desperate for the very person I had been ignoring. Even though my palms were sweaty and my mind was racing, I felt something I hadn't felt recently—peace.

After the event I hurried home and started reading my Bible for the first time in a long time. I underlined Ephesians 2:8–10 and wrote in green ink in the right margin of my Bible, "*Call to destiny.*" It was at once a statement and a challenge. Those words remain there to this day.

In the months following that transformational night, I felt as if I was falling in love again. You know that feeling of giddiness, excitement, and childlike wonder in the beginning stages of a relationship? That's what I felt most, longingly ravished by the love of God and compelled by that same love to do those good works He had prepared for me to do. It was not just about me—my despair and dejection started to fade. It wasn't that I did not think about my sadness; I just thought about myself less and God more.

> By simply saying yes to the right thing or no to the wrong thing, you can change your life forever.

My thoughts were not consumed with how bad life was for me, but rather I began to think about my life's purpose. My life was supposed to be lived for a purpose bigger than myself, bigger than my issues, and bigger than my loss. I wasn't supposed to be cooped up in my apartment, going through the motions, and simply existing. I was supposed to be thriving, not just surviving. I had an unrelenting urge to do something, *anything*, in response to this newfound love for God that I had.

The very first thing I did was get involved in my local church. The local church is indeed the hope of the world and the breeding ground for personal growth in your walk with God. I started attending faithfully, giving obediently, and most importantly, serving others. I volunteered in the youth department of my church, showing up early, staying late, and trying to have a good attitude about it. There was a noticeable change in my life instantly, because the more I thought about others, the less I was consumed with my own problems.

I intentionally surrounded myself with friends who truly loved God and loved me even though I clearly had some major issues. Many of those friends are still in my life today and have helped propel me into the destiny God has on my life. What attracted me most to the church where I planted myself was the fact that it made the prospect of putting God first in every area of my life a reality, not just a wish. In that time God answered so many outrageous prayers I prayed, and I saw many miracles happen in me and around me. I remember a time when I was struggling financially. By struggling, I mean I had more zeroes in my phone number than my bank account. I had just graduated from college, had very little saved up, and was living off a pitiful paycheck.

One particular month I knew that if I tithed, I would not have enough money to pay my rent in full. I felt such audacious faith that I boldly tithed anyway, fully expecting that God would provide for me. The day I was supposed to pay the rent came and passed...nothing! Another day passed, and by the third day I started getting anxious. That night I plopped on my couch dejected. I turned on the local evening news. The lively news anchor mentioned that throughout the broadcast, they would be showing names of people whom the Internal Revenue Service was trying to contact at the bottom of the screen. My ears perked up when I heard that the reason for this was because the IRS was issuing overdue rebates from taxes. My heart started beating a little faster. "Could this be it?" I jumped up and crouched close to my small TV for a better look at the names. I cupped my hand over my mouth and uttered an audible shriek when I saw my name roll across the screen! I could not believe how dramatic this rescue was. I could not peel my eyes away as I watched the rolling news ticker in the lower third of the TV scroll by again and again, each time, seeing my name: Mercy F. Makka. I repeated over and over again, "Thank You, Jesus!"

I woke up the next day and had to pinch myself to be sure that I didn't just dream everything that had happened the night before. I called the appropriate agency to verify the accuracy of what I had seen, and they did. I quickly set up payment of the funds. It was an incredible feeling to know that God had heard my prayers and would come through for me if I put Him first.

GETTING OVER THE "S" WORD

Living my life God's way rather than my way drove the final nail into the coffin of my anger, bitterness, and selfishness. It was contagious. I couldn't help but fall in love with this new life. I was starting to understand that what I had just endured was both the act and the process of complete surrender to God. It did not look and feel like what I thought it would. I felt stronger, not weaker, full of faith rather than fear, and more alive than I had ever been. If I'm being completely honest, whenever I would hear the mention of the word *surrender* or *submit*, I would have a negative, emotional reaction. It's not that I didn't like those words; it's that I didn't like the way they made me feel. Before now, they were simply "S" words in my Christian vocabulary, words I did not care for and certainly regarded with trepidation and suspicion. I still had flashbacks to the things I had seen as a young girl and preconceived notions I had about my identity as a woman. My defensive attitude and hostile posture toward the idea of surrender was rooted in fear. I was trying to compare a biblical principle with worldly experience, and it just doesn't work. If we decide to reject God's way of life because people have abused it, we will miss out on so many incredible blessings God has in store for us. Numbers 23:19 says, "God is not a man, that He should lie, nor a son of man, that He should repent. Has He said, and will He not do? Or has He spoken, and will He not make it good?" (NKJV). God's ways are good and right even when people are not good and right.

I had bought into the lie that strength and surrender can't coexist and that to be an independent woman means not allowing anyone dominate me. This protective mechanism may work when it comes to people, but those rules do not apply when it comes to God. He is a Father who loves His daughters relentlessly. God *is* love. He does not possess love, because if He did that would mean there are times when He does not possess it or is unloving. Love is not something He has; it's who He is. God's love for us is not only the basis of our surrender to Him, but it also removes the fear of it.

Maybe like me you've seen others abused by those who demanded submission to their whim and will. Perhaps you've seen that and vowed in your heart that you will never put yourself in that kind of situation or allow anyone do that to you. It's so easy for our hearts to harden as a result of this, without us even knowing or meaning it to. Then when God comes to knock at the door of our heart we don't even know how to let Him in. The truth is that no matter where you are or what you've done, your life can be much more than what it is right now *if* you surrender it to God. God has infinite power, enough to zap us right now and change our lives instantly, but because He loves us, He has given us free will to choose to allow Him to change us.

However, God can only multiply what we offer to Him. Like the young boy with his sack lunch, or Peter at the gate called Beautiful, or the disciples fishing from their boat in the dark of night, once they released what they had to God, He was able to make it much more impactful to those around them than if they had held on to it. If I want my life to matter, I have to willingly surrender it to God and watch what He does with it. God is all powerful, but we all have the right to choose.

True surrender to God will never diminish who you are; it actually does the opposite. It helps you discover who you really are. I am living proof of this. I lived as a sad shell of myself until I decided to think of myself less and think of God more. In order for me to be who God called me to be, I had to get over myself, get out of my daily routine, start thinking with a new mind, seeing with new eyes, and living with new purpose. My life had so much more meaning once I offered it to God. I love the way A. W. Tozer eloquently pens it: "Only the conquered can know true blessedness."[3]

Jesus understood this stunning truth, which is why He chose to say, "As You wish," in the garden. By choosing that, He was choosing to endure the agony of the cross and in so doing put us above His own desires. He willingly chose you and me. Even when I didn't love Him, when I raged in anger against Him, when I knowingly and deliberately rebelled, when I did things I am not proud of today... even then He chose me. What would be more accurate is... *especially then*, when I was angry at Him, when I chose to reject His offer of having a relationship with Him, He chose me. He chose you. This choosing astounds me.

As I started to build my relationship with God, I began to realize that what He endured for me is even more shocking. He *chose* the path to Golgotha, He *chose* to be silent when ridiculed, and He watched those He loved choose Barabbas over Him. He *chose* to say yes in the Garden of Gethsemane. He *chose* to stay on the cross when a legion of angels could have removed Him from it. Jesus *chose* to surrender. He did not just die *for* me; He died *as* me. His death was as both a representative *and* a substitute—for me.

God loves us and is not a bully. He will never force His way upon us or try to break our will, but rather He woos us to Himself so we can offer ourselves freely and with reckless abandon. Jesus chooses you too, and when you decide to surrender and offer yourself to God, only then can He use you the way He wants to.

Surrendered people are the ones God uses, and we see the lesson of surrender learned in the lives of several Bible characters. Sarah, wife of Abraham, tried to help God and discovered in the end that surrender to God is the only way to go from a promise given to a promise fulfilled. Despite her doubting, Sarah eventually became the mother of all people. Your doubts do not prevent God from using you; a lack to surrender to Him will.

Paul was a furious killer of Christians and by his own admission a "sinner of sinners." One act of surrender changed his entire life and the history of Christianity on his way to Damascus. Acts 9:6 illustrates Paul's heart of surrender: "So he, trembling and astonished, said, 'Lord, what do You want me to do?'" (NKJV). True surrender always presents an opportunity to do something amazing for God, and indeed Paul went on to be one of the greatest Christians to ever walk the earth. Your past won't disqualify you from being used by God, but an unsurrendered life will!

Ruth, from Moab, surrendered to God and found her kinsman redeemer. Queen Esther surrendered to God to the point of being able to state boldly, "If I perish, I perish!" (Esther 4:16). She counted the cost of surrender, measured the risk, and wisely obeyed God despite the risk and the cost, and in the process she saved her people and her life!

Mary surrendered to God and housed the holy of holies in her womb. God chose Mary not because she was the best, most beautiful, or most talented, but because of her spirit of surrender. Look at her response in Luke 1:38: "I am the Lord's servant....May it be to me as you have said." I love the way the King James Version phrases it: "Be it unto me according to thy word." This is the heartbeat of surrender—be it unto us, according to Your Word, according to Your will, according to Your desire. Our hearts have an unending capacity to experience this, and that is God's desire for us.

Chapter Three

QUEEN OF HEARTS

And the day came when the risk it took to remain tight in the bud became more painful than the risk it took to blossom.[1]
—ANAIS NIN

I LOVED BEING PREGNANT with my sweet daughter, Ava-Pauline; I was so thrilled to be having a girl. After having a boy, I was introduced to the brave new world of shopping for girls. All I can say is whoa! The sheer volume of various accessories that girls need can be overwhelming. As I ventured down the pink- and purple-laden aisles at the baby store, I just imagined all the special times I would share with my daughter—braiding her hair, painting her nails, talking about boys when the time came. What I was *not* thrilled about, however, was all the weight I was gaining. To be brutally honest, I was huge. By seven months I was already displaying the duck-like waddle; my feet were puffy and my belly button poked out. I was so obviously pregnant that when people saw me, their spontaneous observation was, "Oh, you're having a baby? You've got that glow, honey!" And I would say, "No, actually, I'm just sweating, but thanks anyway!"

Others were not as kind. They would take one look at my burgeoning belly, gasp, then point and say, "Bless your heart! You look like you're ready to pop! Are you sure there aren't two in there?" Now we all know that in the South when someone says, "Bless your heart," it's not exactly a compliment! I would bite my tongue, restrain myself from saying something unkind, and sweetly reply, "No, there's just one in there."

As pregnant women do, I had some cravings—and not just for weird things, but also for rare things, such as organic goat's milk ice cream that is only sold at specialty stores. My poor husband would drive halfway across town to get me these rare items, such as the goat's milk ice cream and butter mints. Ah, butter mints—a Nigerian candy that is like a marriage between the crisp freshness of a thin mint and the buttery smoothness of a Werther's caramel. I know what you're thinking: sweet genius!

My husband would drive for ten, twenty, sometimes even thirty miles to fulfill whatever new craving I was experiencing. His reward is in heaven for sure! He did all that because he loves me. (Well, to be honest, I also threatened him with bodily injury if he didn't, but that's not quite as romantic!) I'm sure my husband would have much rather been sleeping in his warm, cozy bed at night than getting up to fulfill the cravings of his pregnant wife, but his love for me motivated him to do it.

He was willing to give up something that he wanted for something that I wanted. Love is like that sometimes, isn't it? Sometimes it's demanding, and sometimes it's even risky. You never are sure what love will require you to sacrifice until you are already deeply invested in it. Love is risky. Think about Jesus. He took the risk of loving and ended up being nailed to a tree. Surrender is initiated by and sustained by love.

CHECKMATE

Let's be honest; the idea of surrender is risky. None of us would say we like the feeling of being vulnerable, of being at the mercy of another's will, or trusting another person with our very life.

The enemy lies to us and tells us that the *risk* of surrender is too high for the *reward* for surrender. If we buy in to this lie, it will start to affect us as if it were, in fact, true. The idea of surrender will then become warped and misrepresented in our hearts and minds. So let's look at what surrender is *not*.

1. Surrender is not *giving in*, because when you give in, the focus is still on you. When we think of giving in, it's the picture of someone who is resigned to their fate.

2. Surrender is not *giving up*, like what you do when you no longer want to participate in something.

3. Surrender is not the idea of having tried all other options and, when nothing seems to be working, deciding to give up.

4. Surrender is not the giving up that one party does in a war when they lose and realize there is no chance of winning.

5. Surrender is not the idea of a person with their hands cuffed behind his back, essentially giving up his right to freedom.

The common denominator of all the situations we just mentioned is that you are no longer in control. Something or someone else has forced you to make a decision, or the direness of your situation mandated your choice. But this is not what true surrender looks like.

What surrender should be is a *giving over* of ourselves to God. The focus is no longer on you; it shifts to the one you are giving over to—God. It's not a reactive act; it's a proactive process. You don't do it in order to avoid defeat; you do it in order to secure victory. Jesus willingly handed Himself over. He completely emptied Himself, so that you and I could be free. God did not have to take Jesus's life; Jesus willingly gave His own life over.

What is it that makes us so averse to voluntarily giving ourselves over to anyone else besides ourselves? First of all, perhaps we think it will change who we are if we surrender, that perhaps it might make us a boring, run-of-the-mill, average copy of the original, unique individuals that we are. True surrender to God does not diminish us; it actually does the opposite. It helps us discover who we really are.

Another issue may be that the idea of surrendering makes us feel the one thing no woman ever wants to feel: out of control and *weak*. We are obsessed with the need to be strong, all the time: "I am woman. Hear me roar. Can she do it? Yes, she can!" To believe you must catch every curveball life throws at you with beauty and grace, hair neatly in place, toes manicured, armpits shaved, and adorned in the perfect-size dress and shoes is a *lie*. We weigh ourselves down with the burden of these unrealistic expectations.

> What surrender should be is a *giving over* of ourselves to God....It's not a reactive act; it's a proactive process.

We are godly women trying to be strong for our emotionally weak friends. We are mothers trying to hold it together for our kids. We are wives trying to keep the household running. (Lord knows, our husbands are not designed to do it!) We are career women trying to balance work and family, desperately clinging to the belief that if we just try hard enough, we can *have it all* and we can *be it all*. Pastor and preacher Christine Caine, who has a worldwide ministry and runs a world-renowned organization to combat human trafficking, all while being a wife and a mother of two young girls, says, "He gives us the grace and measure to do and have it all…but maybe just not all at one time!"[2]

We are ruled by ideas such as, "If I don't do it, it's not going to get done." Sound familiar? Embedded in those words is fear—and, strangely enough, pride. "My heart took delight in all my work, and this was the reward for all my labor. Yet when I surveyed all that my hands had done and what I had toiled to achieve, everything was meaningless, a chasing after the wind" (Eccles. 2:10–11).

Startling as it is, pride sometimes hides in humility's clothes. The first time I was asked to preach on a Sunday morning in our main service at church, I thought, "Are you sure You want me to do this? This is the real deal, God. I don't think I can do this." The Holy Spirit whispered in my heart, "You're right. You can't, but God can." Have you ever felt like this? "Oh, little old me, how could I ever do this or that for God?" At first blush that may sound like a humble statement, but there is a big problem with that "little old me" part—the focus is still on *you*. Pride is reliance on our own strength, knowledge, and performance, and it blocks us from enjoying the peace of surrender. If the idea of surrendering to God makes you feel weak…good! It should, because it is at the time when we feel our weakest that God's strength can be made manifest in our lives.

Is Grace Really That Amazing?

The invitation to surrender to God affects us in the most vulnerable part of us: our hearts. For so many years in my life I would do everything I could so as not to feel weak, but it's that very state of weakness through which God is best glorified in us as Christians. People who know me today are shocked to think that I was once a broken, depressed young woman full of anger and bitterness. I put on a good façade for others. I never allowed them to see my weakness. I would do whatever it took: lie, manipulate, and fake it so no one would know how sad and broken I was on the inside. I had this incessant need to feel strong all the time. Maybe you can relate to this. I was always quick to defend my weaknesses, and I worked hard to portray an image of strength, even when I was feeling frail on the inside. As we surrender to God, we will no doubt encounter the fact that our energy is finite and our strength is limited. "Human weakness provides the opportunity for divine power."[3] The problem is that the world has taught us that strength rules and weakness is exploited. Thus, we are suspicious and outright reject anything that would make us feel vulnerable or fragile. In His wisdom God sometimes allows certain things in our lives to expose our weakness so that His grace will be at work in us.

I can identify with that need to feel strong all the time. I was always quick to defend my weaknesses, and I worked hard to portray an image of strength, even when I was feeling frail on the inside.

I am so thankful that the Word of God gives us wisdom for every area of our lives. The verses that set me free from feeling like I have to be strong all the time are found in 2 Corinthians 12:9–10: "'My grace is sufficient for you, for my power is made perfect in weakness.' Therefore I will boast all the more gladly about my weaknesses, so that Christ's power may rest on me. That is why, for Christ's sake, I delight in weaknesses....For when I am weak, then I am strong."

In my study and meditation on these verses, certain words and phrases began to pop out to me. There are five words I would like to unpack using their Greek root words as a road map. Let's build this word by word, phrase by phrase, idea by idea. The first stop is *grace*, in the Greek *charis*, which means "unmerited favor, grace, or divine influence upon a heart."[4] The second is *sufficient*, in the Greek *arkeo*, which means "eliminating a barrier, to defend, or exactly enough."[5] The third is *power*, the Greek word *dunamis*, which means "miraculous, explosive power."[6] This is where we get the word *dynamite*. Fourth, the phrase "made perfect in," in the Greek *teleiotes*, means "completely fulfilled, consummate in character, finish."[7] The root word, *teleo*, is the same as that which Jesus used on the cross when He said, "It is finished."[8] Finally, let's look at *weakness*, in the Greek *astheneia*, which refers to "disease, infirmity, brokenness."[9]

1. My grace = *charis* = divine influence upon a heart

2. Sufficient for you = *arkeo* = eliminating any barriers

3. God's power = *dunamis* = explosive, miraculous, dynamite power

4. Is made perfect = *teleiotes* = completely fulfilled

5. In my weakness = *astheneia* = brokenness

Now let's look at this all pulled together. God's divine influence (*charis*, grace, influence) is exactly enough to meet your every need (*arkeo*, sufficient, eliminates all barriers). For His explosive, miraculous power (*dunamis*, dynamite, turbo boost, Holy Ghost power) is made completely perfect (*teleiotes*, fulfilled, finished) in you when you are broken (*astheneia*, brokenness, weakness) before Him. This is the perfect picture of surrender. One of the main keys to unleashing your true identity is allowing God to expose your weaknesses, embracing them, and relying on His strength to help you accomplish His divine purposes through you. This is what surrendered people do; this is how they think.

Practically it may look different, depending on what stage of life we're in, but no matter how strong we think we are, our strength is limited, and eventually we will run out. Honestly, some of us just need to admit that this is where we are. There's more to life than we can handle, we have too much going on, and we are living with more pressure and guilt than we are willing to admit. We think by working harder, being more productive, being a better _____ (fill in the blank here: person, parent, child, sibling, Christian), we will feel better about life.

Actually we would feel better if we surrendered more to God rather than trying to do more. God can do more in your reliance on Him than you can do in trying harder. If we do less of what we want and more of what God wants, we can achieve more. We get so used to being busy that as soon as we get any margin in our life, we are quick to add something else in there. If we always feel the need to be productivity-driven and continuously push the limit in our lives to see how much more we can take on, we should ask ourselves why.

Personally I struggle with the ever-elusive idea of balance. I don't want to be juggling the things in my life; I want to cradle them. So I have had to schedule times for physical exercise and free time to think and plan. Some days when the stress of my schedule is overwhelming, I just put whatever I'm doing down and take an hour power nap with my kids. Seriously, sometimes the most spiritual thing you can do is take a nap! Remember Jesus in the storm with the disciples in Mark 4:35-41? He grabbed a pillow, went down to the stern, and caught a few Zs. I love it! He understood who was in control so was able to rest even as a storm howled around Him. You were not created by God to have all the ability in your own strength; your strength is intentionally limited so that you can rely on Him more.

> God can do more in your reliance on Him than you can do in trying harder.

Weakness Finder

There is much talk in our social circles about "strength finders" and discovering what you're good at, but I have found in my life that more often it's my "weakness finder" that has served me better. When I feel weak, then I am actually strong. I don't have the strength for my crazy schedule. I am a wife (of a very handsome man, by the way), the mom of two kids (both equally delicious), a pastor at my church (I *love* my church), an author, a speaker at conferences, and wait for it...a part-time nursing professor! Yeah, it's pretty crazy. There are times when I wonder about God's timing, and in those moments I make a purposeful effort to continue to surrender my life to Him completely. I'm sure if I took a peek at your calendar on your fridge or your smartphone it would look a lot like mine. We have hour after hour blocked off for meetings, appointments, extracurricular activities, and the like.

What surrender looks like for me practically is that each day I make my bed an altar—literally. Before my feet ever hit the floor or my kids come in to pry my sleepy eyes open to make them breakfast, I lie on my bed, either supine or prostrate, and pray to God for the wisdom to say "yes" and "no" to the right things and to give the best of my finite time and energy to that day. How we decide to use our time is a good indicator of our surrender to God.

Good time management is a mix of Spirit-led wisdom and realistic planning. We all have the same twenty-four hours in each day; what we do with those seconds, minutes, and hours is what matters. Sometimes it's easier to orchestrate a five-year plan for our lives than it is to plan the twenty-four hours in a single day! Stress is often related to *what* you are doing, not *how much* you are doing. If you find yourself burned out and constantly burning the candle on both ends, it may be because of what you're *not* doing. If you neglect to dedicate time to resting, planning, and study of the Bible, then you will constantly be running on empty. Bill Johnson says it this way: "There must be an aspect to our life that is impossible without divine intervention."[10]

Do you trust God with your daily agenda? It's easy to trust God with things that seem nebulous and far off, such as your future or your calling or your destiny. Trusting God with your daily and hourly agenda keeps you on your edge spiritually and guarantees that you will be "current" in your faith, listening for His still, small voice from decision to decision, hour to hour, and day to day.

The latter is more demanding but infinitely more

impactful. Maybe your day needs to begin in the evening, devoting that time to rest, preparation, and surrendering the day to come to God. As a self-proclaimed night owl, I can identify with this, as I prefer to stay up late than get up early. Those quiet moments in the evening, when my children are safely tucked in their beds, all their toys have been picked up, and the dishes have been washed *and* put away, are some of my most enjoyable and productive. The fact that I work the third shift as a nurse part-time also contributes to my irregular circadian rhythms. Honestly, I chuckle when I read about the Proverbs 31 woman who "rises while it is yet night" (v. 15, NKJV). I think we should all still be sleeping while it is yet night, but maybe that's just me! By surrendering small bits of time faithfully, you can do some big things for God.

At the heart of it, no amount of doing or being will mask the issues in our hearts. If we struggle with inadequacy, no matter how much we are doing or accomplishing, we will never experience the peace and joy that we should. If we trust ourselves with our daily schedules and are afraid to surrender the "little" things to God, we will always struggle. There is no aspect of your life that is too little to surrender to God. The degree to which you surrender the mundane minutiae of your life is the degree to which you will experience the peace of God in your life. You do what you can do. God will do what you can't do.

JUST LIKE YOUR DAD

There is nothing that moves a parent's heart like seeing themselves in their child. I remember after having my firstborn son, I sat in a hospital-issued gown, cradling my baby boy, staring at Isaiah for what seemed like hours on end. I am not sure what I was looking for in his sweet face, but I suspect part of me was looking for something, *anything*, that resembled either me or his dad. "Is that cute little button nose mine? Will his birthmark look like his father's? I wonder whose personality he will have." On and on the questions swirled in my head, because parents are consumed with seeing their likeness in their children. *God is no different.*

We are made in the image and likeness of God:

> For you formed my inward parts; you knitted me together in my mother's womb. I praise you, for I am fearfully and wonderfully made. Wonderful are your works; my soul knows it very well. My frame was not hidden from you, when I was being made in secret, intricately woven in the depths of the earth. Your eyes saw my unformed substance; in your book were written, every one of them, the days that were formed for me, when as yet there was none of them.
> —PSALM 139:13–16, ESV

From these verses in Psalms you can see how consumed and devoted God is about us. This means our hearts were created to be consumed by something. From eternity past to present to eternity yet to come, God's love for us has been consuming Him. He has been chasing us down through the generations. It seems that no matter how much we try to run away from God, He is always waiting, with open arms, for us to come back to Him. We are His crowning achievement, and His desire is to bring us back into right relationship with Him. Our hearts were created to be consumed by something, and if our relationship with

God does not consume us, something else will. Cheap alternatives are even more appealing when you are hungry for something.

This reminds me of an occasion when I was a newlywed and eager to please my husband with a hearty, homemade steak dinner. I knew he would be home from work around 6:00 p.m., so I timed everything perfectly. I marinated the T-bone steak with rosemary and garlic, then grilled it well done, just how my husband likes it, with a medley of summer vegetables. Then I started on the homemade steak fries, peeling, cutting, and frying them by hand. Now you know it's true love when you make homemade fries from scratch rather than getting the frozen ones from the store!

I anticipated the look of surprise and gratitude my husband would have on his face as he walked through the door. But I never got to see that look because when my husband came home, he saw the spread on the dinner table and uttered a miserable "Oh, no." I thought maybe he didn't like what I had prepared, and I quickly offered to cook something else, but that wasn't the problem. He told me that he was so hungry on his way home from work that he stopped by McDonald's and grabbed a Big Mac with fries and a milkshake—and he wasn't hungry anymore. I disappointedly packed up my gourmet, homemade steak dinner in Tupperware. "I guess I'll be packing myself a steak dinner for lunch tomorrow!" I thought to myself.

Our hearts are hungry for God. They were created to be passionate, so if we don't fill that desire with God, then something else will happily take His place. If you don't

> You are free to choose what you will surrender yourself to, but you are not free from the consequences of that choice.

fill your heart with the right things, you will be enticed to overindulge on an inferior substitute. Most of us would not knowingly settle for a previously frozen burger in place of a homemade steak dinner, but hunger can skew your judgment and distort your decision-making skills. What are *you* hungry for? Have you chosen to overindulge in something other than healthy spiritual food? Choose wisely when it comes to what you will allow yourself to surrender to. You are free to choose what you will surrender yourself to, but you are *not* free from the consequences of that choice.

Chapter Four

THE FEAR FACTOR

The remarkable thing about fearing God is that when you fear God, you fear nothing else, whereas if you do not fear God, you fear everything else.[1]
—OSWALD CHAMBERS

ONE SUMMER MORNING a few years ago I flung open the tan curtains in my living room as I do every morning; it's part of my wake-up routine. As I was gazing out my porch door, staring at the pond by our backyard, I thought I saw movement out of the corner of my eye. I did a double take and didn't see anything out of the ordinary, so I shook the curtains again, and sure enough, a brown, hairy, monstrous rodent raced to the corner of my house and disappeared under the love seat. All I felt was fear...and also nausea...but mostly fear.

Instinctively and in one smooth motion I scooped up my six-month-old who was playing nearby and leapt onto one of our end tables with speed and alacrity. I wish you could have seen the dexterity and nimbleness with which I did this. I can attest to the popular saying that rodents, spiders, and snakes have been making impromptu athletes out of women from the beginning of time. I detest any household pests with a passion, especially disease-ridden, foul rats. In fact, when God gave us dominion over every creepy, crawly thing, I am willing to bet that He was mostly talking about rats, spiders, and snakes. OK, maybe that's a little bit of a stretch...maybe. Today, my foe was a rat, and I shouted at the top of my lungs when I saw it.

My husband came bounding down the stairs to see me screaming and pointing. "We have a rat, and where there's one rat, there are always more rats!" Like a loving husband should, he took care of the situation, and we eventually got rid of all the rats. But if I can be honest, every time (and I do mean every single time) I open the curtains, part of me is extra-vigilant to look for any vermin. Our minds are naturally conditioned to be afraid—no one has to teach us to fear heights, strangers, or pain.

There is nothing so paralyzing in the process of surrender like fear. Fear is a prideful way of thinking that you have more control over the circumstances of your life than you actually do. Think about it! We all fear something! Instead of fearing God, many of us fear the wrong things in life. We fear snakes and danger, heights and water, getting old and growing fat.

- Many of us fear failure, but how many of us fear the God who never fails?

- Many of us fear abandonment, but how many of us fear the God who never leaves us forsakes us?

- Many of us fear loneliness, but how many of us fear the God who never leaves us alone?

- Many of us fear pain, but how many of us fear the God who endured the pain of the cross?

- Many of us fear death, but how many of us fear the God who overcame death and the grave for you and for me?

I still remember the terror I felt in the waning moments after losing my mom. "What if someone else I love dies? What if I die? What if I never feel happy again?" On and on the mental torture went, and eventually I started to live in fear. The real issue was not so much that I was afraid of the future; it was that I was not in love with God in the present. I did not allow His love to infiltrate my heart and protect me from fear. Oswald Chambers is right. When you fear God, He releases you from all other fear. Perfect love casts out fear, and you will serve whom you fear. If you fear man, you'll serve man. If you fear God, you'll serve God. This was a truth I *knew*, but I had not yet appropriated it into my life.

Even years after I lost my mother and brother, I still felt the sting of betrayal and disappointment, so it was hard for me to accept and trust God's love. Considering what I had just endured, loving God fully seemed pretty risky to me. I started to think, "If I really give God all of my life, then what else will I have to endure?" My love for God was now associated with a question mark. "How long? How far? How much?"

Surrender to God asks you to commit to something when you don't know how far it will take you or how much it will cost. Until I was no longer in control of its cost, I could not demonstrate love to its fullest. It would be like going into a relationship while filling in the following blank: "I will love you until _____." This is not a good way to enter into a relationship with people—or a relationship with God.

Selfish love says, "I need to see exactly what this relationship will require of me before I can fully commit." At any point in a relationship based on selfish love, you can back out if you feel it's costing you too much. That would be like walking down the aisle on your wedding day with the idea of divorce as on option if things don't work out. It almost dooms a relationship to come into it with a lack of trust and commitment. True surrender turns such thinking on its head, because trust is essential for surrender to take place.

Surrendered love says, "I will love you without any conditions on that love." This kind of love exposes itself to what that commitment will be, even if it costs more than you can configure. Now I understand that you may read that and think, "That's just too hard for me to do. How can we love anyone without conditions? We're not perfect people." You're right; we don't have the capacity in us to love like that—but God does.

It would be really hard to let love motivate us to surrender without holding back *anything* if we were doing it in our own strength. But we don't have to try to do this on our own. "And hope does not disappoint us, because God has poured out his love into our hearts by the Holy Spirit, whom he has given us" (Rom. 5:5).

With the help of the Holy Spirit, God will give us everything we need for life and godliness, including living a life full of the kind of God-love that expresses itself in true surrender to God. First John 4:18 tells us that "perfect love drives out fear," so we can trust the love of our Creator. Perfect love comes from a God who gives only good gifts. This kind of reckless and radical love is trustworthy because it comes from the "Father of the heavenly lights, who does not change like shifting shadows" (James 1:17).

Surrender, like salvation, is also a soul issue. It is not automatic; it's a voluntary, decisive response to something. If you respond to fear, you will not find the motivation to surrender, but if you respond to love, you will. Most of us naturally yield to fear, but we must deliberately yield to God. The questions to ask is this: Are fear and lack of trust in God taking over your life, or are you willfully laying them down in surrender? It's always going to be one or the other. If you choose to respond to fear, surrender will not be a way of life for you. If you choose one, you are automatically rejecting the other.

Our soul is our mind, our will, and our emotions. The best part of surrender to God is that it's not a one-way deal; it's part of an equation. We give Him our broken, messed-up souls, and He gives us eternal life. We give Him our addictions, and He gives us freedom. We give Him our sickness, and He gives us healing. If you're like me, you read that last sentence and thought, "Well, God doesn't always give us something better in return. Sometimes people don't get healed. Sometimes they get even sicker and die. So then what?" This is a valid question, one that I asked myself many times in the years after I lost my mother. I had to tackle the root of the issue, which was fear.

The biggest distraction and obstacle to surrendering your soul is fear. Perhaps this is what you fear most about surrendering to God and giving over control of your life, that you will somehow come up empty. To give over your soul can sound overwhelming and offensive. To surrender your soul may sound as if you'll give up everything and get little back in return. I have been in that place, mourning the death of my mother and wondering if I could truly surrender my soul to God. I still don't have the answers as to why God allowed it to happen, but even when things are beyond my understanding and comprehension, they are not beyond my trust. God is God, I'm not—and I'm thankful for that.

There are some things I will never understand on this side of eternity, questions that will go unanswered until I stand before Jesus face-to-face. My questions will not dictate my faith; God's love for me will! I love how Rick Warren states it, "I would rather walk with Jesus with all my questions, than walk without Him with all the answers."[2] We must allow God's love to drive out fear because when you love the Lord your God with *all* your mind, *all* your will, and *all* your emotions, it's difficult for fear to creep in and overcome you. When you choose love, then by default, you are rejecting fear.

PAY THE PRICE

It was my freshman year at the university, and I was filled with giddy anticipation and youthful fervor. I would lie on my twin bed across the room from my roommate, and we would take turns dreaming up steamy scenarios of how we would travel the world, experience new adventures, and have romantic dates with our boyfriends. We designed and strategized: Which outfits worked best? Should we wear this jewel-toned accessory with those high-heeled pumps? Should we buy new clothes? On and on we planned. None of my stories about the boyfriend part ever materialized, however, because I received an ill-fated phone call from my boyfriend, and you can probably predict how this melodrama played out. The conversation did not go well; it was punctuated with awkward pauses and an almost palpable distance between him and me. Nobody lingered on the phone, no sweet nothings were uttered, and then he said the dreaded phrase, "It's not you, it's me." I flinched at that. "At least don't use a cliché," I thought. "I deserve an original breakup line at the very least!"

My dreams screeched to a halt, and I was left with the fragments of a broken heart. When you're nineteen, everything is the end of the world, and this really was

> The biggest distraction and obstacle to surrendering your soul is fear.

the end for me. I made several rash, preposterous, and outlandish vows, many of them starting with the words "I will never again…" In my emotional outburst, I uttered a promise to God that turned out to be one of the most life-changing experiences I have ever had. I told God that I would not date anybody for at least one year and instead dedicate that time to my relationship with Him. This was a decision made out of pain as much as purpose.

In retrospect my intentions were pure. I just had no idea what I was getting myself into by making such a vow. Many times before that year was up, I mourned the fact that the Second Coming would happen, the Rapture would be upon me, Jesus would roll back the clouds like a scroll, the trumpet would sound, and I would stand there and realize that I had not experienced marriage—and of course, sex!

I watched my friends date, and I lived vicariously through them, like a bridesmaid who never gets to be the bride. "Oh, you and your boyfriend are backpacking through Europe? That's great." "What? You're engaged! Wow, your three-carat princess-cut diamond is blinding me. Congratulations!" I was missing out on all the fun and thrills of young collegiate love. To make matters worse, about four months into my vow it seemed there was no shortage of tall, strapping, and gorgeous specimens of the male variety. (When I look at the man I eventually married, I realize I look for the same things in men that I do in chocolate: dark and sweet!)

Faith sometimes asks you to do something in advance that will only make sense in hindsight.

I can't describe to you how difficult it was to turn down the advances of the very thing my heart desired: to be loved by someone, to be chosen, to be in a dating relationship. And I didn't have the guarantee that those opportunities would still be there at the end of my yearlong vow. I was experiencing the fear of "What if when I'm done with this vow I won't have anyone interested in me?" That thought haunted me because it's the feeling of vulnerability when you have let go of something without yet laying a firm hold on something else. It is like the feeling you would have if you jump from one side of a deep chasm to reach the other side. There is a moment when your feet have left the familiar ground, but you have not yet landed safely on the other side. It's a scary, vulnerable feeling. That was exactly how I felt during this time in my life, and it required me to have faith in God.

At the time it made little sense to those around me. My friends would ask, "Are you sure you'll find someone after the year is up? What if you don't get anyone else like this guy? What if you end up single, old, and lonely?" The truth is, they were not asking me anything I had not already thought about in my own head. It really did not make much sense, and I could relate to their confusion. There are times when trusting God does not always make sense. Faith sometimes asks you to do in advance something that will only make sense in hindsight. It was giving up something in the present for another thing that was yet to come.

It truly was the Holy Spirit who enabled me to say no when all the other girls in my world were saying yes. Did I feel awkward and left out? *Yes!* Did I sometimes feel as if I was wasting the prime years of my life? *Yes!* Did I struggle with my identity and insecurity? *Yes!* Was I afraid that I would never get married, one day realizing I had become a crazy cat lady? *Yes!* Did I say things to God such as, "If You want me to be single and just adopt kids later, that's OK with me," secretly hoping reverse psychology would work on God? *Yes!*

When my emotions threatened to overwhelm me, I did the only thing I knew to do—spend a significant amount of time studying, reading, and meditating on the Word of God. I did not set out to live a holier-than-thou life. It's just that when you remove the temptation that comes with dating in your late teens and early twenties, there's little else to hinder your walk with God. I had to be motivated by a passion that did not originate from my fleshly desire or lust. In my low points I would mourn the things I could not do, all the things I had to say no to, and how much I was missing out on. On the upside, when I allowed my relationship with Jesus to bring me joy and I saw how much I was growing spiritually, life seemed so much simpler.

In paying the price of saying *no* to relationships for a season of my life, I was choosing to say a massive *yes* to God in a way I had never done before. In order to do this, I had to overcome some major fear. I felt God calling me to a higher standard, to pay the price for daring to be different. Different is not always easy, and it's certainly not popular, but it *will* stir up your faith and force you to trust God.

Not giving it up

I believe one of the ways the enemy attacks this generation of young people is by convincing them that they should be afraid of paying the price to be different. They believe that the price is too high, so they settle and conform to the world. If you're a young person reading these words, know that the church needs you and your generation to be the church of today, not the church of tomorrow. The world desperately needs your voice *now*, your authenticity, your creativity, and your passion.

It grieves my heart when I'm at a mall and see what the marketing world thinks our young girls want to see. I watch them proudly carrying bags displaying a picture of a half-naked guy on it, and I have major problems with this! There is a systematic, sophisticated attack on young people. Social media and the Internet age have introduced a whole new arsenal against them.

When I see how things are shifting in our world, how the things that can be shaken are being shaken, I am even more convinced that our young people are specifically and strategically gifted to be the hope of our ever-darkening world. When God needed to birth the Messiah, He used the womb of a young girl to carry His Son! He's still in the business of using young people to change the world!

The world has skewed the idea of celibacy and made it seem archaic and old-fashioned when it actually is a gift. I remember in middle school, we had a True Love Waits campaign that encouraged us to commit to waiting for marriage to have sex. We all enthusiastically signed up for the abstinence campaign and received silver rings with those words inscribed on the inside.

I remember my friends and me signing True Love Waits pledge cards. We jokingly compared ourselves to roses and said we didn't want to keep giving away petals to different guys and then have nothing left but thorns to give to our husbands. Back in high school in the late '90s it was fairly common to be celibate until marriage—even applauded.

By college most of the girls who took that pledge had already given it up, and only a few of us could still say we were virgins. When you're in your late twenties and told people you were still a virgin, you could get some strange looks. I can only imagine that when you're in your thirties, people stare at you as if you're an alien from outer space. They have that look in their eye that says, "Yeah, right, no way!" The petal and rose allegory is only cute for a little while, and it can only be used for so long.

Young people need to know that God is not against sex. He is for marriage. He does not want you to be secluded from others or socially awkward. He does want you to be completely, 100 percent devoted to Him. That's hard to do when you have baggage and emotional distress from relationships. For me, my season of celibacy was marked more by my total, all-out devotion to God rather than what I didn't want to do. Before I was married, it was more about saying yes to God than saying no to sex. If you're single, I encourage you to devote this season to God rather than pine for what you don't have. It is a gift. Time is your most precious resource, so don't just spend it; invest it.

I see many young people, especially young girls, so distracted by the fear of being alone that they get desperate and settle for the wrong guy and the wrong relationship. Instead of being the unique, confident women God created them to be, young girls are investing in the wrong relationships, wrong thinking, and wrong beliefs. They are trying to be like everyone else, date like everyone else, talk like everyone else, listen to the music everyone else listens to, and dress like everyone else.

Young woman, your beauty and charm was not given to you for flirting, manipulating, or enticing men. That insecurity you feel about yourself cannot be satisfied by a cute outfit or by a dating relationship. Insecurity can only be satisfied by one man—God! The problem is that we have God-size problems, and we are looking for man-size answers. Guess what? It doesn't work! Even if you never had a father figure in your life, God is the *only* man who will never leave you, never disappoint you, and never let you down. You can trust Him.

You were bought at a price—consecrated and set apart, body, mind, and soul. If you understood this, not just in your head but in your heart, you would never willingly let anyone devalue your body. Your love for God would trump the fear of being alone, and you would not settle for just any guy. Jesus paid the highest price anyone could pay just to have a relationship with you, and this should make you view yourself differently. A young woman who knows she is a princess would not deal with a peasant. If you understand that the presence of the living God resides in your body, you would not settle for a one-night stand with some stranger. We need to understand that our sexuality was given to us by God, and in order to have the fullest joy, peace, and satisfaction from it, we have to have relationships following God's guidelines.

The enemy knows that you have legitimate privileges associated with your body. He also knows that God created sex to be a powerful union between a man and a woman when God's image is expressed in its fullest expression. What a powerful image! One gender can't express all God is; we need both male and female, in the sanctity and unity of marriage. Marriage is the only context for sex; anything and everything else is sin. Period. Full stop. The end. There are no fifty shades of gray. God put those desires there, and He, not the world, tells us how to express them so we can be blessed.

The enemy knows that when we surrender our sexuality to God, we will experience blessing and satisfaction beyond what we can imagine. His bait is to get us to access what already rightfully belongs to us, either before it's time or in the wrong way. Just like a trust fund that can only be accessed at a legal age, expressed sexuality is a privilege that can only be legally accessed under the marriage contract. Solomon warns us not to stir up or awaken love until it pleases (Song of Sol. 2:7). When you access it before it's fully mature, you will miss out on the full benefit of it.

The bait of the enemy is to tempt us to prematurely access what will only be legitimately ours in marriage. If we take the bait, we sell ourselves short and miss out on the blessings of God. We also stunt our spiritual growth and discover that something that should leave us feeling fulfilled and complete leaves us feeling empty, ashamed, and guilty instead. The enemy's tactics are not new. He tried to do this with our Savior.

Remember when Jesus was being tempted by the devil in Matthew 4? Jesus had been fasting for forty days and forty nights and was, understandably, hungry. "Again, the devil took him to a very high mountain and showed him all the kingdoms of the world and their splendor. 'All this I will give you,' he said, 'if you will bow down and worship me'" (vv. 8–9).

At this point Jesus, being fully man, had two options. He could either take the enemy's bait and gain premature rule of the world, or He could remain surrendered to God and obey the will of His Father. Imagine the

There is one thing that both God and the enemy know about you; you are a prevailing and powerful force on the earth

74

effect on the world if Jesus had chosen to do the former, given up His sinless life and forfeited becoming the Savior of the world. Jesus eventually received from His Father all that Satan had offered Him, but He was willing to pay the price to do it God's way, which included going to the cross first. If the enemy tried it with Jesus, he'll try it with us—you can count on it!

Our defense is the same as the one Jesus used: wielding the Word of God as a sword and walking in surrendered obedience. Those two weapons will extinguish any fear the enemy heaves at our hearts. There is always a price to pay for surrendered obedience. Are you willing to pay the price even when it's not easy, popular, or convenient? It may cost you your reputation, popularity, friends, or social status but the end result will be worth it.

There is one thing that both God and the enemy know about you; you are a prevailing and powerful force on the earth. God sees your life as a solution to a problem on the earth; the enemy sees your life as dynamite power that needs to be defused and neutralized. An extraordinary woman who has shaped my life immensely, Lisa Bevere, says it this way: "The attacks on your life have much more to do with who you might be in the future than who you have been in the past."[3] We have to understand that some of those attacks can come in the area of relationships, and who we choose to be in relationship with has an immense impact on our lives and our destiny.

Many surrendered Christians maintain unsurrendered relationships and justify it with love. This is especially true for young adults. We let our natural emotions supersede our spiritual inclinations—a very dangerous zone to try and navigate. We sometimes choose to limit how much control God has over this particular area of our lives. The devil does not have to kill you; he just has to bring the wrong relationships into your life and convince you to conform and compromise. Don't be afraid to pay the price to be different; surrender your sexuality to Him. God wants all of us, not just some of what we choose to give to Him.

Chapter Five

ALMOST DOESN'T COUNT

All to Jesus, I surrender, all to Him I freely give. I will ever love and trust Him, in His presence daily live. I surrender all, I surrender all.[1]
—JUDSON W. VAN DEVENTER

LOVE SPORTS. I am definitely the kind of girl who is intensely competitive with a "go big or go home" kind of mentality. My husband and I love being outdoors and active, and we will occasionally play tennis. Whenever I lose a point or a game, I get animated, talking loudly to myself and blurring the line between being encouraging and demanding. One particular day, as I started my verbal complaints about the fact that I lost a game, my husband grabbed the neon yellow ball we had been playing with, flashed a wry smile at me, playfully shook his head, and said, "Babe, I think you actually hate losing more than you like winning." I am inclined to agree with him.

As a prepubescent, middle-school girl I was gangly and awkward with really big feet. Much to my chagrin I was also a bit of a dork. I was the nerdy girl whose favorite place was the library, hidden behind a stack of books, reading the latest Judy Blume book, searching for another classic by John Steinbeck, or lost in the magical world painted by J. R. R. Tolkien's *The Hobbit*.

Thankfully I was also gifted athletically and excelled in sports. I loved how popularity and sports seemed to go hand in hand. My competitiveness and agility were a formidable combination in basketball and volleyball, my favorite sports. In middle school I would sit on the edge of the jagged cement steps by the open air courts at school and watch the varsity players, dreaming of the day I would be in a red jersey on the court representing Hillcrest High School.

When that day finally came and I made it to the varsity basketball team, it was everything I dreamed it would be. I loved winning, and I loved being on a team. But there was another aspect to being on the team that I hadn't seen from the edge of those cement steps. What I did not see when I watched the varsity players competing, winning championships, and basking under the accolade of their accomplishments was *what it took to get there.* I did not see the sweaty two-a-day practices beginning at 6:00 a.m. I didn't see the hours and hours of weight training and gym work that they faithfully put in. I didn't see them running suicides (I think the concept of a practice drill aptly named a "suicide" is self-explanatory).

My basketball coach contrived an evil plot where every girl on the team would shoot two free throws, and we would have to run a suicide for every free throw missed during practice. I am pretty certain that idea originated from the pit of hell (yes, in hell there is weeping, gnashing of teeth, and running suicides). In addition to practice we sometimes had tournaments on a Saturday morning while our other classmates were probably sitting on the couch in fleecy pajamas watching cartoons and eating Corn Pops.

I quickly realized that I did not like adhering to a strict curfew on Friday night to prepare for a Saturday morning game while my friends stayed out late having fun. Little did I know that being on the team meant getting up early and staying up late to practice. It meant taking time to study our plays, to practice shooting for hours on end, and to get up for early workout sessions. Then there's all the homework you still had to do after practice and before school the next day.

There were times when I wanted to give up, but I didn't because I was inspired by my love of the game and the girls I played with. I knew there would be consequences if I failed to do those things, because our coach always said, "Ladies, if you practice hard, you'll play hard." She challenged us to put in as much effort on the practice court, running drills and studying plays, as we would on game day. She almost always ended her pre-game speech with a variation of this phrase: "Ladies, play like a team. Go all in because almost winning doesn't count."

ALL OR NOTHING

This got me thinking. In our surrender to God, we have to go all in, push all the chips to the middle of the table, wave the white flag of our rebel hearts, put both our hands up, and hold nothing back. Anything short of that is not good enough. Almost surrendered, almost devoted, almost faithful—this is not good enough for God. If you were to jump out of a plane and your parachute *almost* deployed, the consequences would be dire and probably fatal. In college, almost passing a test could be the difference between moving on to the next year or having to repeat a class. Even though it may seem small when you're making the decision, there is a big difference in the *outcome* of being all in and being almost all in. Imagine if a friend says they almost accept you, or if your parents say you almost make them proud, or if your child says they almost love you. This falls far short of our expectation and leaves us feeling empty and hurt. Imagine standing before God and instead of God saying the words we all want to hear—"Well done, good and faithful servant"—you hear these words uttered from the mouth of Father God: "Well, you were *almost* faithful. You *almost* became who I created you to be. You *almost* fulfilled your destiny." How tragic would that be?

We simply cannot use our faith as an excuse for mediocrity. Calling yourself a Christian and striving for anything less than your best will not please God. I find that we tend to compartmentalize where we strive for our best. For example, we work with excellence in ministry or at our jobs, but our social life is out of order. Or we bring our best to our friendships, but our home is in disarray or our finances are out of order. We should function at our best in every area of our lives. Our goal is not perfection; it's to maximize the use and potential of *everything* we have been given by God.

One area I am challenged in as it relates to functioning at my best is physical fitness. How well I take care of my body is just as important as any other spiritual discipline I take on. Staying physically fit in high school and college was relatively easy and convenient. This is not the case now, after having two kids as well as facing all the job, home, and ministry responsibilities I have. There are many days when I don't stick to my eating plan or don't have enough energy to go to the gym or for a run. I am tempted to be hard on myself, which leads me down an emotionally negative path, and on it goes in a downward spiral. I have only one physical body, and it is a vehicle for me to fulfill my God-given calling. I have a responsibility to take care of this gift He has given me, and anything less is not my best. I am not looking to be a certain size or fit into a certain pair of jeans; I am looking to keep *my* body in the best physical shape possible so I have the energy I need to love my husband, raise my children, and continue to preach the gospel.

> Our goal is not perfection; it's to maximize the use and potential of everything we have been given by God.

I am still as competitive as I was back in high school.

The main difference is that I have two things now that I didn't have then: perspective and maturity. My goal is not to be better than anyone else; my goal is to be like Jesus. I have since learned that failure does not need to be devastating. I don't like to fail, but I can handle it; I understand that the world will not stop rotating on its axis because of my performance. My passion for performing at my best originates from a place in my heart that seeks to be my *best* self. It was a motivation to extract the most out of my body and do the most with what I have been given by God. To know I could give 100 percent of my energy on a court, win or lose, but yet not do it would feel hypocritical. It's the same idea with our faith; we need to go all in and not settle for mediocrity. We should not try to be average when we're created to be great. Total surrender to an almighty God does not ask you to settle for ordinary when God created you to be exceptional.

SET APART

Think about the life of Samson, who was called by God in his mother's womb. Before he was even born, an angel appeared to his mom, and he was set apart by God to be a Nazirite. Samson was "the man," and the Spirit of the Lord was upon him mightily. God equipped him with supernatural strength to help deliver his nation from the Philistines. Mixed martial arts stars have nothing on Samson: he tore a lion apart with his bare hands, killed a thousand men with the jawbone of a donkey, and judged Israel for twenty years.

So how on earth could such a young man of promise be seduced away from his purpose and not even realize it was happening? The seducer of our souls always acts consciously and deceptively to put us in a position of vulnerability and weakness, with the ultimate goal of destroying us completely. Much more than sexual misappropriation, seducers can come in the least suspicious forms, and all seduction finds its roots in a lie.

Your seducer may not be a person; it may be your selfish desires, your craving for approval, or your desperate need to be loved. Your seducer may even be comfort in the culture around you that is contrary to the Word

> My goal is not to be better than anyone else; my goal is to be like Jesus.

of God. Think about what Samson was reduced to in Judges 16:21: powerless, purposeless, and hopeless. He had once been lauded as the hero of a nation, but he was now a prisoner, chained up, walking around blindly grinding grain. Many sources claim that the Philistines burned his eyes until they were liquid and then scooped them out. What happened? How did our champion become a chump in such a short period of time?

Samson was an incredibly strong man with an incredibly weak will. When you put that lack of a strong will in the context of being emotionally driven, you have the recipe for a catastrophic moral failure. *Almost* does not happen all at once, though; Samson did not wake up one day and decide to forfeit his Nazirite vow. It happened little by little, decision by decision, day by day.

Although God had plans for him to deliver His people from oppression, Samson chose not to go all in with his Nazirite vow and he became an almost; he *almost* kept the vows God gave him; he *almost* became who God called him to be, *almost! Almost* is not all in; *almost* doesn't count; *almost* happens in small steps, and an *"almost surrender"* is an oxymoron. The devil has the same intentions for us that he had for Samson; he wants to remove our vision, chain us up, and have us walking around in circles looking crazy!

As my pastor Stovall Weems says, "We all pay a price. Either we pay the price of obedience or we pay the price of regret." Samson ended up walking around in circles, blind, full of questions and regret. He paid a costly price for settling into the culture around him, allowing a bad relationship to grow, and never fully going all in with God's plans for his life. It's easy to look at Samson's life and see the mistakes. We have the benefit of hindsight for that, but what about your life? Where are the areas of compromise? What are those habitual sins we think are little but turn out to be big? Delilah was not the first Philistine woman that Samson entangled himself with. She was the third, according to Judges 14:1 and 16:1. Not only that, Samson violated his Nazirite vow to the Lord long before the moment Delilah lulled him to sleep in her lap and had his seven locks of hair shaved off (Judg. 14:8–9). He had gone down the slippery slope between sin and disobedience so long before that he had no idea the anointing of the Lord had departed from him.

May that never be our story, that we go through our lives never fully surrendering to God thinking we are living a "good" life when in reality, God is not the Lord of our lives. What price will you pay—the price of obedience or the price of regret? It's not too late to move from the

> This is the incredible mercy and grace of God: you are one decision away from full surrender to God and turning your life around.

camp of *almost* to the camp of *all in*. This is the incredible mercy and grace of God: you are one decision away from full surrender to God and turning your life around.

The best part of the Samson's story is this: "But the hair on his head began to grow again after it had been shaved" (Judg. 16:22). It is never too late to surrender completely to God no matter what failures and mistakes are in your past. God loves to give us a second chance so that we are without excuse.

We could all give excuses as to why we can't go all in for God and why our past mistakes disqualify us. The truth is that at the end of our lives, when we stand before God, excuses will not be good enough. Even the heroes of our faith had excuses. "Abraham was old, Jacob was insecure, Leah was unattractive, Joseph was abused, Moses stuttered, Gideon was poor, Samson was codependent, Rahab was immoral, David was a murdering adulterer, Elijah was suicidal, Jeremiah was depressed, Jonah was reluctant, Naomi was a widow, John the Baptist was a 'weirdo,' Peter was impulsive and hot-tempered, Martha was OCD, Thomas had doubts, Paul was a killer of Christians, and Timothy was timid."[2] Each of these people went all in for God, and He used each of them to do something significant in the world. He will do the same for you no matter your past. You can have faith in the finished work of Jesus on the cross that no matter what you have done in the past, Jesus paid the price for it, and it's as far as the east is from the west.

Chapter Six

PIG THEOLOGY

Self-sacrifice through self-control is necessary for self-fulfillment.[1]
—RHONDA H. KELLEY

I WAS SPEAKING AT a women's conference and conversing with the other speakers before the beginning of the service. One of the women stood out to me. Her story and life so captivated me that I was in tears before the conference even began. Gail McWilliams sees life very differently than most. Her monumental struggle was in an area that most of us experience routinely: having a baby.

Gail tells the story in her autobiography, *Seeing Beyond: Choosing to Look Past the Horizon.* Gail and her husband, Tony, had the desire to have children and to see their legacy continue, but they had complications due to Gail's struggle with childhood diabetes. The doctors had told them they probably would not be able to have children due to complications from the disease, but they chose to have hope anyway.

Gail tells her incredible story this way: "Our hope gave birth in time to five miracle children the doctors thought it would be impossible for us to have. During my second pregnancy, a pattern of risk to my eyes became clear. I had diabetic retinopathy. The blood vessels in my eyes hemorrhaged during pregnancy. The doctor surprised me one day with the ultimatum, 'Gail, you must choose today between your baby and your eyes.' I quickly said, 'I choose my baby.' The doctor stood to his feet as he angrily shut my file. 'What a foolish decision,' he said, and then left the room.

"As I sat alone, stunned by his reaction to my choice and unaware of the winding, dark road ahead of me, I remembered a passage of Scripture I had buried in my heart since I was a young girl. 'I have set before you life and death, blessing and curses. Now choose life, so that you and your children may live' (Deuteronomy 30:19). The

Giver of life had helped me make the right decision in a moment of crisis."[2]

What a touching and heart-rending moment in her life! Gail's decision inspired and challenged me. She knew that she was making the right decision in God's eyes, and she was completely committed to that decision, even if it meant she would lose her eyesight. Even though Gail ended up being blind, not only did she have that child, but she also went on to have three more children! Today Gail's children are all living lives full of joy and purpose. The same child the doctor advised her to abort has presented Gail with her first grandchild.

Of course, there is a sorrow in not being able to see her sweet grandson's face, but Gail made a decision to love God and love her children no matter the sacrifice. What a beautiful picture of surrender.

Passionate Surrender

We must not underestimate the power of our decisions. How you make decisions, especially hard ones, says a lot about whether you have surrendered to God. Sometimes this requires complete sacrifice, and other times we may have to make seasonal sacrifices in order to go beyond involvement to commitment. Surrender has to go from what we know in our hearts to the decisions we make in our minds and what we do with our hands and feet.

Prosperity and comfort, more than poverty and inconvenience, can dull our spiritual vision. Are you sacrificing where you need to in order to fulfill your commitment to God? Gail chose life. She chose to put God first: above her desires, above her dreams, and even above her eyesight. Surrender forces you to make a decision about whether God is first in your life or if something else has that place. God must be preeminent. He cannot be second; He must be first.

I read this analogy somewhere and it stuck with me: "When you look at a plate of ham and eggs, you know the chicken was *involved*. The chicken gave something of little sacrifice (the eggs), but the pig was *committed*. The pig gave everything, its very life." The chicken gave *something*; the pig gave *everything*. That may be a little humorous, but there is much truth in it.

Many Christians have a chicken mentality when it comes to giving, serving, and loving others. We give until it starts to hurt. We serve until it becomes inconvenient. We love until we are asked to do so selflessly. We bring this same mentality to surrendering to God. We give God some of us, part of us, but not everything. It is the difference between just being involved in your relationship with God and being committed. It's going from being familiar with God to being intimate with Him. Familiarity is not intimacy; surrender inspires you to want to become intimate with God.

Prosperity and comfort, more than poverty and inconvenience, can dull our spiritual vision.

It is one thing to be a chicken-Christian—you're involved, you give something of little sacrifice, but you stop short of letting the cost become more than you can bear. It's another thing to be a pig-Christian—you're surrendered. You've given everything to God. Let's be pig-Christians! Let's not just give *something*; let's give *everything*.

Think of Jesus! He wasn't just involved with what happened on the cross of Calvary; He was committed and surrendered! He didn't *almost* go to the cross of Calvary, and He didn't *almost* wear a crown of thorns; He fully bore the weight of the sins of the world, including yours and mine.

When Jesus was asked what the greatest commandment in the law was, He said, "Love the Lord your God with *all* your heart and with *all* your soul and with *all* your mind and with *all* your strength" (Mark 12:30, emphasis added). I love how *The Message* phrases it: "The Lord your God is one; so love the Lord God with all your passion and prayer and intelligence and energy." The phrase "with all your passion" pops out to me. The way we bridge the gap from involvement to commitment is to stir up our passion for God.

Have you ever met people who are unapologetically passionate? They are infectious and inspiring. I think of Olympic athletes who train for years to perform for a few days, sometimes even a few minutes, every four years. They adhere to a strict diet, training, and exercise regimen just to compete. I remember reading about an athlete who said she gave up eating dessert for two entire years as she trained for an Olympic relay race. Now *that* is passion!

Passionate is how God wants us to feel about Him, because that is exactly how He feels about us. God's greatest desire is that we reflect His passion toward us, back to Him. When you dig deeper into the word *passion*, you will find that the Greek words *pascho* and *pentho* mean "to suffer."[3] *Passion* is not a word relegated to daytime soap operas and romantic movies. An accurate picture of passion is not a couple swinging from chandeliers in a dreamy love scene. If you watched the movie *The Passion of the Christ*, then you know that the passion that fueled our Lord was not pretty and flowery and neat. Passion means to suffer; it's sometimes brutal and always self-sacrificing. It means you are willing to suffer for something, to inconvenience yourself for it. This is the antithesis of our modern-day culture, which puts a premium on ease, convenience, and drive-through anything! We love our fast-lane checkout at the grocery store, our fast-pass tickets at Disneyland, and anything microwaveable. We get so conditioned to ease that any stimulus that causes exertion or strain on us seems foreign and feels strange.

Sometimes learning begins with unlearning; that is, we have to break down our old thought patterns and beliefs about suffering, because in order to know Jesus and the power of His resurrection, we *must* share in the fellowship of His suffering. This means we are more like Christ in our suffering than we can dare to imagine. Until we can put to death our selfish need for everything to be convenient and easy, we can never be like Jesus.

Remember Gail's story? She gave up something she loved, her sight, for something she loved more, her children. She has had to share in Christ's suffering in a tangible way. God is not able to enjoy relationship with some of the children He died on the cross for. Some of His children actually reject the opportunity to have a relationship with Him. It is tragic that Gail is not able to see the very children she gave up her sight for, but in so doing she is sharing in suffering.

Gail does not feel sorry for herself, and she assured me, when I spoke with her, that although her eyesight may be impaired, her vision is keen. Gail has a radio program, and she travels all over the world speaking and inspiring others as she did me that day. She is living out her passion to reach others with the love of Christ. Gail is also very funny, peppering the delivery of her life's experiences with humor and candor in a way that makes you fall in love with her that much more.

SUFFERING AND SMILING

In Nigeria we have a saying for when things are not going your way but you are enduring through it; we call it "suffering and smiling." I love this because it speaks to tenacious faith that acts in advance of what is yet to come. It's the kind of faith that sees beyond the present trouble for a day when you will smile again. But this faith does not wait for that day, no, while the suffering is still going on, your faith has matured to a place where you can smile as you suffer. Gail's life shows this, she smiles through her blindness, and it shows her passion for God. She affirmed what I knew in my heart but her story illustrated beautifully. The fact that God allows suffering in my life does not mean that God does not love me, that God is not with me, or that God does not have a perfect plan for me. The fact that my mother was not healed should not make me doubt God's ability to heal or His desire to heal.

Our trust in God is not dependent on whether He answers our prayers or not; trust is based on faith. Gail's faith had grown through the process of having to trust God so completely while being in the dark. There is something about suffering that produces a faith that can be trusted. A faith that is tested by fire is a faith that can be trusted.

A faith that endures the fiery trials of life is a faith that can be trusted. So here is a question for you to wrestle with: Can your faith handle the painful silence of unanswered prayers? If we are being completely honest, many people's faith can't handle a faith challenge because they have faith that relies more on what God does rather than who God is. When you have to go through difficult times, it reveals what is in your heart and what condition your faith is in. Can your faith handle the trial of an unanswered prayer? Let's say you pray repeatedly and incessantly, and you believe with everything in you that God will answer that prayer—and He doesn't. Can your faith handle that? What about personal loss—loss of possessions, loss of your health, loss of someone whom you love?

What happens when you want to conceive a child and you can't, or when your child is born and then doesn't live? How do you react to God when you suffer?

> Our trust in God is not dependent on whether He answers our prayers or not; trust is based on faith.

Gail mentions that she has witnessed other people receive their sight while she still remains blind. Her faith does not waver because God has performed many other miracles in her life, including the ability to have children. Her faith is not tied to God giving her back her sight, although she hopes that one day, either on this side of eternity or the next, she will receive her sight again. Her faith is tied to the fact that she can passionately say, "God is good," and she means it. This kind of faith is what surrender develops in us.

In Acts 16:23–26 Paul and Silas had endured a brutal beating and were thrown into jail for preaching the gospel. Even as their feet were yet in stocks they were praying and singing hymns to God. Verse 26 says, "Suddenly there was a great earthquake, so that the foundations of the prison were shaken; and immediately *all* the doors were opened and *everyone's* chains were loosed" (NKJV, emphasis added). Did you catch that? It wasn't just Paul and Silas's chains there were loosed as a result of their faith in God and praising Him in the midst of their suffering. The chains of everyone in that prison were loosened! Even in your suffering, there are seeds to someone else's comfort. Your trial can be the spark for someone else's joy, and your struggle can bring inspiration to one who desperately needs it, if only you will endure it.

Love the Lord your God with *all* your passion. Passion is bravery in the face of danger, steadfastness in the face of opposition, action in the face of resistance, and optimism in the face of despair.

Passion says, "Fear won't stop me, I won't back down, I won't be intimidated, and I won't lose heart." You will have courage for what you are passionate about, and you will be willing to suffer for what you are passionate about. Passion looks less like a steamy scene from a daytime soap opera and more like the grisly, bloody, beaten body of our Savior on the cross of Calvary. Passion looks less like, "I *have* to do this for God," and more like, "I *get* to do this for God." Passion understands that sacrifice hurts but also that the presence and Spirit of God always fall on a sacrifice.

BOLD AND BEAUTIFUL

One of my favorite heroines in the Bible is Queen Esther. She is my kind of "shero," stunning yet powerful, confident yet humble, and determined to make her life matter. There is enough drama in her story to rival an episode of *America's Next Top Model* or any modern fairy tale. Pixar or Dreamworks could make some money depicting this tale!

Imagine the scene in your mind: a displaced, orphaned Jewish girl reared by Mordecai, an older relative. She enters a beauty contest to take the place of the rebellious and deposed Queen Vashti. There is a gathering of all the most gorgeous young virgins at Shushan, the citadel (Esther 2:8). All these fair maidens are then put through an elaborate twelve-month beauty makeover and spa treatment for the ages. This makeover included six months of sitting around a small charcoal fire pit in the floor with fragrant oils such as sandalwood, cloves, myrrh, or rose heated with fire. Another six months of perfume, an ancient beauty process from the Persian period where the young ladies sat by the fire and perspired, exfoliated and opened up their pores in order to absorb the fragrant oils and perfume. (See Esther 2:12.)

Esther makes every cut in the running to be the next queen and rises to the top of the contenders. She even garners favor with the custodian of all the maidens and is elevated to a place of honor and eventually chosen as the next queen (Esther 2:17).

Mordecai informs Esther that the Jewish people have a date with extinction, a plot masterminded by the wicked self-promoter Haman. The plot climaxes here. Esther is faced with fear: she could either devise a plot to save her people (which meant risking her life), or she could do nothing. She could go all in and risk everything to save her people or settle for an average, nominal life. Mordecai's words were certainly ringing in her ears: "For if you remain silent at this time, relief and deliverance for the Jews will arise from another place, but you and your father's family will perish. And who knows but that you have come to royal position for such a time as this?" (Esther 4:14).

Her response shows how resolute and unwavering she was in stepping into her destiny despite the risk and the cost. "Then Esther sent this reply to Mordecai: 'Go, gather together all the Jews who are in Susa, and fast for me. Do not eat or drink for three days, night or day. I and my maids will fast as you do. When this is done, I will go to the king, even though it is against the law. And if I perish, I perish'" (Esther 4:15–16).

Sometimes passion is not sensible or safe in the way we normally view it. It seems like the sensible thing for Esther to remain silent and play it safe. It was common knowledge in Esther's day that the protocol was to wait for the king to summon you before you approached him. If anyone approached the king without being summoned, they would die unless the king extended his gold scepter to spare their life.

By planning to seek an unrequested audience with the king, she was almost certainly sealing her own fate and giving up her life. Esther was well aware of this, uttering those legendary words: "If I perish, I perish." Those are words of courageous determination, not an expression of resignation to the inevitable. This is the power of passion; it gives you strength when you need it most. I truly believe God allows certain events in our lives to bring faith and passion out of our lives in a measure we did not even know we had.

Esther had to have felt paralyzed by fear. I'm sure she was tempted to give up or give in, but courage told her no. She stepped into her destiny even though it meant great sacrifice and likely death. She seized the right moment, presented her case, humbly asked for the Jews to be saved, and won the ear and the respect of her royal husband. I particularly love the fact that God was able to use every part of who she was to accomplish His plan for her life. God used her beauty, her charm, and her intelligence, *as well* as her passion, her remarkable courage, and her fearless nature to accomplish His will. She lived up to her name and indeed became a "star" in her generation.

SMALL DETAILS, BIG RESULTS

Now our own picture of going God's way instead of our own way may not involve a life-and-death situation. Your decision to go all in for God may not be as dramatic or climactic as Queen Esther's. It is actually seldom that way; it's usually the little things that tell the tale of whether we are all in or not, whether we have truly surrendered or not. It's the small, seemingly insignificant things that scream out the loudest.

Deciding what television show to watch, which friend to call, what to do with your time, how to organize your day, how you discipline your kids, and how you react when you're angry, all of these say a lot about the condition of your heart. What you do when no one is looking is a better picture of your heart of surrender than what you do when everyone is looking.

These little details, seemingly mundane and ordinary, can lead up to a life of surrender. It is the little things that prepare you for making the big decisions. It really is the little things that count. Think of those little decisions as a whole lot of little things that add up to a whole life over

> Your life will not change until you change the voice you listen to and trust.

time. The difference between just being involved to being committed can be found in the little things.

It is striking to me that the voice Esther chose to listen to affected the outcome of her life. Be careful whose voice you listen to. I am sure Esther heard a lot of voices telling her to give up, give in, back up, back down, or backslide. I am certain she heard the words, "Who do you think you are? You're just one person. You're just a girl; what can you do all by yourself? How can one woman change the world?" Esther chose to listen to the voice of her cousin, who perceived her moment of destiny.

Your life will not change until you change the voice you listen to and trust. The very fact that God chose you out of eternity and you are now existing means that you were also were born for such a time as this. We make the call of God something mysterious and complicated when it's really quite simple. How do you know that God has a call on your life? You were born! The proof of God's calling on your life is that you are alive, so seize the moment and go all in for God.

Esther could have been just a young queen and lived her life in the shadows, but this was her moment of destiny, and she rose up and was confident in the call of God on her life. God does not need us, but He chooses to use us. Our sovereign God will accomplish all His objectives with or without us. He calls us not out of His need for us but out of our need to find fulfillment in serving Him. Make the decision today. Go ahead, be a pig!

Chapter Seven

SURRENDERED YET POWERFUL

There is an essential difference between submission and surrender. The former is the conscious acceptance of reality. There is a superficial yielding, but tension continues.... It is halfhearted acceptance....There remains a feeling of reservation, a tug in the direction of non-acceptance. Surrender, on the other hand, is the moment when my forces of resistance cease to function, when I cannot help but respond to the call of the Spirit.[1]
—BRENNAN MANNING

My husband, Marcus, and I are a perfect example of how opposites attract. He's quiet; I am loud and boisterous. He's an engineer and a genius at math; let's just say I scored higher in English than math on all the standardized tests I took in high school. His first language is French; mine is English. My husband shows restraint and great strength under control. Sometimes I am a little out of control. My husband is a peace-*maker*; I am a peace-*keeper* (note the subtle difference between those two).

In fact, during our premarital counseling sessions with the pastor who married us, we did a little survey where we answered a few questions about our preferred method of resolving conflict. After the series of questions, we were assigned an animal that represents how we resolve conflict. According to that questionnaire, when it comes to our natural instincts in resolving conflict, Marcus was a turtle while I was a shark!

We *are* compatible in all the areas that make a marriage wonderful: our relationship with God, our desire to help each other achieve their God-given purpose, and our love for our family and friends. I remember telling someone, "We don't fight about the big issues because we agree on all the big issues."

A few months into our new marriage, I brought up an issue that was bothering me, something trivial such as putting a new roll of toilet paper on with the edge pointing down (because, let's be honest, that is the *only* way to load a new roll!). The discussion turned into a heated argument and quickly escalated. The tempo of the conversation increased, and new subjects started being tacked on.

At this point, the volume and anger in our respective

voices intensified. How could our nuptial bliss have hit such a low point so fast? The harder we tried to resolve the issues, the further we were from a solution. Finally Marcus shot me a blank stare and said, "I guess we'll just have to agree to disagree." I replied with a terse "Fine!"

The next few days were edgy and uptight. We still went through the same motions, but it was indisputably a cold war. I gave him the silent treatment, and he made sure we were never in the same part of the house for a prolonged period of time. If I was upstairs, he found a way to be downstairs. If he was in the kitchen, I would find something to do in the den. We were like ships passing in the night, filling up the silence between us with small talk and niceties about household chores—talking without connecting.

My heart was heavy because I knew I needed to apologize to my husband for the things I'd said. Knowing is only part of it; I knew what to do, but I just did not want to do it, simple as that. I didn't want to admit I was wrong because I wanted to make a statement. I wanted to be right, and I wanted him to apologize for being wrong. For the first time in my marriage I felt that my identity as a strong, independent woman was tied to my need to be right, my need to have my own way, and my need to assert myself. If I gave in, then I wasn't strong, because giving up was the same as admitting defeat. And if there's one thing I don't do well, it is admitting defeat!

I kept having these conversations with myself in my head, vacillating between the desire to be right and the desire to be at peace with my husband. At the end of it all, I just could not take the tension anymore. I waited for an opportune moment and quietly approached my husband.

I then said these two words and meant them with all my heart: "I'm sorry." That was all it took. Order and peace were restored in my home.

DEADLY DESIRE

If you're a wife, then this scene, or one similar to it, has probably played itself out in your home at some point. The truth is our surrender to God should also reveal itself to our submission to the people God has placed over us. Submitting yourself to another person is easier said than done. The truth is that the moment you surrendered your life to Jesus, you also willingly accepted submission to the authority God has placed in your life. Marriage is a crucible for the testing of our character and identity as women.

The very idea of submission can be offensive because by its very nature it creates a desire in us to resist it. There is a desire in us to protect ourselves from being hurt, being taken advantage of, and being controlled. This desire expresses itself as stubbornness, selfishness, and pride. Feminism, at its extreme, is an affront to the order God has placed in our families.

Perhaps you would not categorize yourself as a radical feminist; maybe you don't go around burning your bra or staging protests for female world domination. However, I am willing to bet you have felt the effects of Genesis 3 at some point in your life. After the Fall of man, God said, "Your [Eve's] desire will be for your husband, and he will rule over you" (Gen. 3:16).

Therein lies the conflict, our desire; this is the root we must attack. The cause of this desire in us is the same source that caused Eve to, in one solitary moment, believe the lie of the enemy that God was anything less than good.

As Eve did, we sometimes decide that we, rather than God, know what is right for us. What makes us do this? The answer is simple: *sin*. Eve decided to choose her way and was cursed from that day on. Her curse still lives on in us, in our natural inclination to rebel against authority.

God did not give us the desire to rebel; all He gave us was the freedom of choice. Once we chose, then our desires became a consequence of that choice. Have you ever been driving and noticed to the right side of the road that the speed limit displayed is thirty-five miles per hour—and then you instinctively push your foot on the gas pedal just a little more? It's almost as though there is something inside of you that makes you want to test the limit and see if you can get away with going thirty-eight miles per hour. Seeing the thirty-five mph limit did not *create* a desire in us to test the limit. That desire was already there; the sign just *revealed* it. The fact that the governing authority is asking us to adhere to a speed limit does not give us the desire to push the limit; that desire is already deep-seated in our hearts.

This same thing happens in us when we run into something or someone that tests our rebellious nature. Personally, this happened to me when I got married. My new circumstances revealed blind spots in my heart. I honestly did not realize how selfish and stubborn I was until I got married and began to have children. When I decided to marry my husband, I was plunged headlong into a covenant relationship that was not conditional. My submission to him is not based on his behavior, his expression of love, or

> The only thing that can redeem us from the curse is the very thing we are resisting: surrender.

even his actions. It's based on my surrender and obedience to God.

When conflict arises, the fact that my instinct is to try to push my agenda and get my way is a reflection of the condition of my heart. Learning to submit to the authority of my husband in marriage does not cause me to rebel. That desire is innate. It's a preexisting condition. It was there when I was single, and getting married did not magically make it go away. The more I reject submitting to the authority in my life, the more tension there is. Submission is not the problem; my wrong desires are.

The only thing that can redeem us from the curse is the very thing we are resisting: surrender. The more we surrender to God and submit to others, the more that part of us that loves to rebel dies. Surrender feeds the part of us that is after God, wants more of God, and desires to live in unity with others. When we submit to those God has placed in our lives to protect us, such as our husbands, it brings joy to our marriage, it highlights the beauty of genuine love, and it is a testimony to the world around us.

DOUBLE DUTY

We submit to others and surrender to God. If you can't submit to others, how can you surrender to God? True surrender manifests itself not only in your relationship with God but also in your relationship with others. Submission still holds a tension; I choose to submit and always hold that choice in my hand. Surrender, on the other hand, removes that tension; it's a giving *over* rather than a choosing.

Both are necessary and essential if we are to become the people God has created us to be. If you're like me, you might be wondering, "So how can I give myself over and still be the strong individual God has called me to be?" Aha! This is the mother of all mysteries, because I can bet strength is not the first image that pops into your mind when you hear the word *surrender.*

This is a major roadblock for most people, especially women, as we put surrender and strength at odds with each other. The two are not mutually exclusive. Surrender is not an absence of strength; it is humility in the presence of strength and the ultimate expression of strength under control. There is no doubt that we, as women, have been endowed with authority from God, and we have been given more opportunities to exercise our God-given authority and leadership than any time in history.

William Ross Wallace beautifully penned this sentiment in one of his poems: "The hand that rocks the cradle is the hand that rules the world." The authority women have to impact and influence generations to come is astounding. The dictionary defines *authority* as the power or right to give orders and influence others to obey or to take specific action. Authority is usually conferred upon a person by someone of a higher rank. We know that the Bible says in Matthew 28:18 that all authority in heaven and on earth has been given to Jesus Christ and that same authority was conferred upon us when we received Christ. Authority is conferred or delegated. You don't *take* authority; you are always *given* authority.

How can surrender and authority coexist? Jesus said He could do nothing apart from His Father in heaven. The very key to His authority on the earth lay in direct relation to His surrender to God. It was not His *title* of rabbi that gave Him the authority to cast out demons, to heal the sick, to forgive people of their sins; it was His *surrender*! If you refuse to surrender to the authority God has placed in your life, you are refusing to walk in the fullness of the power conferred on you by the government of heaven.

The truth is, spiritual authority is based on relationship, not position or title. The title you carry—stay-at-home mom, single college student, full-time ministry worker—is not what gives you real authority. Your spiritual authority is based on the intimacy of your relationship with God and the fullness of your surrender to Him. If

Surrender is not an absence of strength; it is humility in the presence of strength and the ultimate expression of strength under control.

you are looking for a title or position to help you figure out your identity and authority in Christ, you will be disappointed.

Look at the story of the sons of Sceva in Acts 19. They were the sons of a Jewish chief priest who saw and envied the power that Paul had to cast out demons and perform miracles. God was working some amazing and unusual miracles through Paul, "so that even handkerchiefs and aprons that had touched him were taken to the sick, and their illnesses were cured and the evil spirits left them" (v. 12). The seven sons of Sceva wanted the power Paul had, but they did not first have the relationship with Jesus that Paul had. Needless to say, it did not work out well for them. They tried to use the name of Jesus to cast out demons. Acts 19:15–16 narrates the story this way: "[One day] the evil spirit answered them, 'Jesus I know, and I know about Paul, but who are you?' Then the man who had the evil spirit jumped on them and overpowered them all. He gave them such a beating that they ran out of the house naked and bleeding."

First of all, you know it's going to be a tough day when evil spirits are talking back to you! Second, we may chuckle at that story, but I can't help but think, does heaven look at the church of today as the sons of Sceva sometimes? Do we ever grab hold of Jesus's name and run into battle unprepared? We wield a religious title over true spiritual authority. We carry it around like a banner, flashing Bible verses and claiming power by name alone, and we get torn apart by the enemy.

If your life is one full of activity that leads to burnout without intimacy with Jesus, then this may be a wake-up call for you. There is no title as important as follower of Jesus. No stage beckons as brightly as the one you kneel in front of rather than stand upon. Let us not go from activity to Christian activity, from conference to Christian conference, and from event to Christian event without understanding what deserves the best of our energy and attention. Let us not be so busy ministering *for* God that we forget to minister *to* Him. Let us live a life that is consistent with what we teach and preach. It all starts with intimacy with the person of Jesus, and then everything else will flow naturally and beautifully out of that.

TAKE ME TO THE CROSS

One of my favorite old choruses says, "Turn your eyes upon Jesus, look full in His wonderful face, and the things of earth will grow strangely dim in the light of his glory and grace."[2] Jesus is both our example and our focus when we talk about living a life of surrender. He walked in power, authority, and surrender. Perfectly. To live a life of true surrender is to be Christlike. Surrender says, "Less of me, more of God."

Power does not need to be exerted in order for it to be effective. Think about Jesus on that cross. He had access to all the power in the world, to the entire arsenal of angel armies, the very dynamite of heaven, and yet He chose to limit Himself. Just let that sink in for a moment; every single supernatural act—every healing, every miracle, every resurrection from the dead, every demon-possessed person set free, and every salvation—Jesus performed as a human being. "I tell you the truth, the Son can do nothing by himself; he can do only what he sees his Father doing, because whatever the Father does the Son also does" (John 5:19).

Every single supernatural act—every healing, every miracle, every resurrection from the dead, and every salvation—He did everything not because of some superhuman capacity, but by His *choice* to surrender and submit to God and through His dependence on the power of the Holy Spirit. Jesus had power and influence, yet He willingly limited Himself, like a dove whose nature is to fly freely but willingly surrenders itself to the laws of gravity and stays grounded. Jesus had to depend on the leading of His Father so He could fulfill His purpose on earth.

Philippians 2:5–8 says, "Have this attitude in yourselves which was also in Christ Jesus, who, although He existed in the form of God, did not regard equality with God a thing to be grasped, but emptied Himself, taking the form of a bond-servant, and being made in the likeness of men. Being found in appearance as a man, He humbled Himself by becoming obedient to the point of death, even death on a cross" (NAS). Jesus did not grasp His equality with God even though He had every right to, He released His grip; He let it go. This is surrender.

Time after time, decision by decision, He chose to surrender His will to God's will, and this was the key to His exploits on the earth. If we do this, John 14:12 will become a reality in our lives: "I tell you the truth, anyone who has faith in me will do what I have been doing. He will do even greater things than these, because I am going to the Father." What? How can we possibly do greater things than healings and resurrections? Through the empowerment of the Holy Spirit who came to us after Jesus left to go to the Father. Our world desperately needs those of us who call ourselves Christians to walk in this kind of power.

In God's world surrender puts you in a place of authority, but in order for us to lead well, we must follow well. Verses 9–11 of Philippians 2 show us this about Jesus, saying, "For this reason also, God highly exalted Him, and bestowed on Him the name which is above every name, so that at the name of Jesus EVERY KNEE WILL BOW, of those who are in heaven and on earth and under the earth, and that every tongue will confess that Jesus Christ is Lord, to the glory of God the Father" (NAS). Jesus's authority is directly linked to His submission and obedience to God.

Bill Johnson says it this way: "For authority to be expressed, there must be subjection. And if there is to be subjection, self must be excluded."[3] The self is that part of us that seeks its own way. My father spent over twenty years in the Nigerian military and retired as a four-star general. From his early years he learned you have to take orders as a recruit before you can give them as a four-star general. A leader cannot become a leader until he learns to follow. It is the same with us. We must learn to be submitted to God's direction in our lives on a continuous, day-by-day, hour-by-hour, and moment-by-moment basis. God gives authority only to those who have an awareness of their own incompetence. We must humble ourselves to be exalted and used.

I have a friend who is a key leader on staff at a prominent, growing church. She is a high-capacity wife, mother, and administrator. I am amazed at how humble she has remained, even while shouldering the burden of making decisions that affect the entire church significantly. She told me once, "If I am not willing to clean baseboards and plunge toilets, then I'm not worthy to sit at the table with the top leaders. I am not here to look important or be significant. I just want to serve people and please God." I love the way my pastor, Stovall Weems, says it: "We are not leaders who serve. We are servants who have the privilege of leading."

This is the best way to navigate the obstacle of balancing the tension between wanting recognition for our abilities while yet submitting to the leaders we are under. Leadership and submission go hand in hand; they actually potentiate one another. The more we are able to submit, the better we will be able to lead.

We need to resist the temptation to overcompensate and try to convince others of our competence and giftedness. First of all, it is not our mandate to change people's minds about women in leadership and places of authority; only God can do that. Hebrews 13:17 gives us some sound advice: "Obey your leaders and submit to their authority. They keep watch over you as men who must give an account. Obey them so that their work will be a joy, not a burden, for that would be of no advantage to you."

HEART AND SOUL

God has placed people in our lives as authority figures to teach us how to submit. Who are the authority figures in your life? Perhaps it's a parent, a teacher, a pastor, a spouse, or a boss. Learn to appreciate them and respect them. Do not disregard the things they say and the influence they try to have in your life. Submit to and publicly honor the leaders you have been placed under. They may not always do the right things or lead in the right way, but if at any point there is conflict, refer back to the Word of God for direction and instruction. It is possible to disagree with someone in authority without dishonoring or disrespecting them.

In AD 54–68 Nero ruled Rome and was a diabolical emperor who ruthlessly persecuted Christians. There are stories told of how Nero would dip Christians in hot wax, set them on fire, and use them as lighting for his gardens. It was when this same Nero was in power that Paul penned these words in Romans 13:1, "Let every soul be subject to the governing authorities. For there is no authority except from God, and the authorities that exist are appointed by God" (NKJV). If anyone had a reason to not submit themselves to the authority over them, it would have been Paul in Rome at that time! Yet Paul did not do this; he exhorted the believers to submit to that authority because it was ordained by God.

I also find it interesting that Romans 13:1 says "every soul," not every person or every one but every soul. Our soul (mind, will and emotions) must be in submission. So if you're having some submission issues, maybe you need to do a check of your heart and soul. Get your emotions in check, shed light on the matters of your heart, and regain control of your will. Most of the issues we have with surrender are heart issues.

We're to be diligent—above all else—in the care of our inner man before God. "Above all else, guard your heart, for it is the wellspring of life" (Prov. 4:23). Solomon is advising us to pay careful attention to our hearts. I remember going over to a friend's house and looking on the side of her fridge as I went to get a glass of water. Her fridge had many of the things all of our refrigerators display: grocery lists, pictures of family and friends, children's artwork, and her monthly calendar. As I peered closer at all the activities lined up for each day of that particular month, I saw all the usual things you might find on a calendar. She was a busy working mom with doctor appointments, parent-teacher meetings, birthday parties, bridal showers, and the like organized by color and category.

> What we do in the limited time on earth affects where we will spend a limitless, eternal existence.

One activity did catch my eye, though. On one particular day she had something circled and highlighted in pink; it said "self-breast exam." Now, if you knew my friend, you would not find this at all surprising; she is an adventurous, fun-loving, "party in a bottle" kind of woman. She is very health-conscious, paying particular attention to what she eats and always looking for ways to be more physically active. I love that she prominently displayed it for all to see what kind of attention she gives to the health of her body.

We should give the same quality and quantity of attention to our hearts as we give to our bodies. It's confounding to me how much time we spend taking care of the outside of our bodies; indeed, companies are making billions of dollars in profit because of this! If I were to ask you what one area of your body you would like to improve, I think the answer would be quick and right on the tip of your tongue. I am guilty as charged in this area, as well. I literally cannot go past a mirror without at least checking myself out once. I have spent plenty of time standing in front of the bathroom mirror going over all the surfaces of my body with an imaginary surgeon's scalpel, imagining all the different areas I would like to nip, tuck, lift, and trim.

However, I understand that all my physical body does is house the real me; it is of no eternal significance, and I don't get to take it with me to heaven. The parts of us that are on a constant trajectory into eternity—our hearts, our souls, and our spirits—should get as much, if not more, of our time and attention. What we do in the limited time on earth affects where we will spend a limitless, eternal existence.

We have elaborate advertising campaigns to remind us to check our breasts, and while I am all for being proactive about our health and primary prevention, no matter how fabulous your breasts are, one day gravity will take over. They may even look like flip-flops by the time it's all said and done! In what I fondly refer to as my BK (before kids) days, I took great pride in my taut, fairly muscular abdomen. Two kids later my stomach looks like bread that had every intention of rising but had a last-minute change of heart *plus* stretch marks. I think we can all identify with the sad transformation that takes over our bodies: what used to be a smile line has now become a wrinkle; what used to be muscular is now saggy; what used to be firm is now flabby. If you have no idea what I'm talking about, give it a decade or two *or* have a child or two, and you will be able to relate to this much easier. It's just the way things go. You can't beat gravity.

Our bodies deserve some, but not all, of our attention. When was the last time you turned the mirror inward and performed a heart check, really examining the nooks and crannies of your inner person? Be honest with yourself and ask the tough questions: Why don't you want to submit your will to your spouse, boss, or parent? What script is playing in your head and mind? Do you have some control issues that need to be exposed? Are you harboring any unforgiveness toward others or offense toward God? It might be time to do a heart check.

Chapter Eight

GLORIOUS RUINS

All God's revelations are sealed until they are opened to us by obedience.... The tiniest fragment of obedience, and heaven opens and the profoundest truths of God are yours right away. God will never reveal more about himself until you have obeyed what you know already.[1]

—OSWALD CHAMBERS

MY HUSBAND AND I went on a cruise vacation with stops in Belize, the Cayman Islands, and Cozumel, Mexico. We had planned for months to go on this vacation and were excited that the time was finally here. We boarded the cruise ship, got comfortable in our room, and then explored the ship. If you've ever been on a cruise, then you know that the best thing about cruises is the fact that you can eat all day, every day, anytime you like. You can fulfill any food dream you may have: pizza at midnight, ice cream for breakfast, pancakes for dinner, whatever suits your fancy.

The first stop on the cruise was the Cayman Islands, and it was a breathtaking sight. The clear water beckoned with fish darting right through our feet as we stood at the shore. Their vibrant orange, blue, and purple hues shimmered and gleamed underwater. It was a bright, sunny day, and we slathered ourselves with creamy sunscreen throughout the day. We had so much fun snorkeling, swimming, and just relaxing on the beach.

The next day our cruise ship stopped in Cozumel, Mexico, and I noticed it was an overcast day. The sun would peek through broken clouds from time to time, but mostly it stayed hidden behind the clouds. Even though it was still hot, because it was cooler and partly cloudy, I decided to forgo the sunscreen for that day. We had a wonderful time in Cozumel, boarded the ship at the end of the day, and had a fun night at the captain's dinner banquet.

When I woke up the next day, I felt sharp, stinging pains across my shoulders and back. Thinking maybe I had slept in a bad position, I tried to stretch out my back and found that I was peeling and shedding like a snake shedding its outer skin. Then it dawned on me. *I had a sunburn!* In fact, I had the worst sunburn I have ever had, and I was genuinely shocked. *How could this happen?*

After doing a little research, I found out that ultraviolet light, the kind that can be dangerous and causes sunburns, has greater penetration than visible light, so even when you can't see the sun, the ultraviolet rays can still harm you. Under partly cloudy conditions a phenomenon sometimes called the broken-cloud effect can come into play, resulting in higher UV levels than a clear sky would produce, and so there was an even greater risk of sunburn. I had let my guard down, I stopped protecting myself, I let myself be exposed, and I got burned.

PROTECTION FACTOR

Offense is a sneaky thing. It takes root in our hearts before we have time to see the signs or even diagnose the symptoms. After I lost my mother, it took me months to figure out that I was actually offended by what God had allowed to happen in my life. I thought I just was mad at life in general and maybe at other people. I was shocked to realize that my offense was really most directed toward God. Offense will reverse and suffocate anything in your heart that is willing to surrender to God, especially when you are going through a difficult situation.

Suffering and hardship can cause us to let down our guard, allowing offense to creep in. We can end up getting burned by it. Matthew 13 shares a parable about a person who hears the Word of God, receives it with joy, but then falls upon hard times and on stony places. Verse 21 says, "But since he has no root, he lasts only a short time. When trouble or persecution comes because of the word, he quickly falls away." The King James Version of the second part of that verse says, "When tribulation or persecution ariseth because of the word, by and by he is offended."

My heart experienced this very thing. As a Christian I genuinely loved God, but when trouble came, because my roots did not go down deep, I became offended and stumbled. My offended heart stunted my spiritual growth and poisoned my relationship with God and others. I remember that if I heard that anyone got healed or shared something positive that was going on in their relationship with God, I could not be happy for them. In fact I would be cynical and skeptical. Ever done that? How you react when someone else gets the very thing you're asking God for is a good indicator of whether or not your heart is offended.

Offense poisons our relationships with people and hardens our hearts. Our hearts are supposed to be soft, like a precious metal. Gold, when it's pure, is soft, but when it's mixed with another substance, it becomes an alloy and is no longer pure. Then it becomes hard and difficult to mold. Hardened gold is much easier to break than soft gold. This is a good picture of an offended heart, gold that is no longer pure.

Guilt can also breed offense. If anyone has ever lost a loved one, then you know that guilt is a major part of the grieving process. I had said some things to my mother that I regretted, and I had also left some things unsaid that I wish I could now say. I thought of ways I had failed her, all the ways she had sacrificed so much for her family, and I marinated in that guilt. I simply could not forgive myself for not seeing the medical signs sooner, not taking

> Offense is deception from the enemy who always seeks to corrupt our view of God.

her health issues more seriously, not knowing how dire the situation was that night. "If only I had done more...I should have done more."

I can't tell you how many times those kinds of thoughts went through my head in the months and years that followed. I almost could not let go of the guilt even if I wanted to because it made me feel better to feel bad about it. I know that sounds absurd, but it's true. In some twisted way, I felt I was giving due honor to my mother by not letting it go, by not forgiving myself, and by blaming God. It's crazy how your heart can deceive you. Feelings are at best fickle and at worst dangerous. My guilt infected my view of God like a virus invades and takes over a body, infecting the good cells so that eventually they turn against the body to do harm instead of good. The same heart that used to feel love toward God now feels anger; the same lips that uttered praise spew blame and criticism.

Offense is deception from the enemy who always seeks to corrupt our view of God. Think of Eve in the garden. This is a woman in a perfect, utopian paradise. All she's ever seen is love, beauty, and the absence of evil. Yet somehow the enemy was able to convince and deceive her into thinking that God was selfishly holding something back from her. How was he able to pervert the character of God in her heart to the point that she believed the lie? This is not an accurate view of God. When we surrender to God, it forces our roots to go down deep as we become more mature in Christ.

Surrender relieves us of the need to always understand exactly what God is doing and how He's going to do it *before* we can obey. Our minds are trained to look for the tangible in the intangible, the visible from the invisible, and the temporal in the eternal, which leads to frustration and disillusionment. Our spirit, on the other hand, is perfectly in tune with God's Spirit when we surrender to Him. The Holy Spirit guides us into all truth, but accept that some truth is beyond our human comprehension. Make no mistake about it; your surrender to God will be tested. Maybe it hasn't been yet, but rest assured it will be at some point.

Lily's Story

I met a sweet fifteen-year-old girl when I went on a mission trip to Zimbabwe. We will call her Lily. She was beautiful, with deep-set hazel eyes set against skin the color of tea with a hint of milk. Her curly locks framed her round face, and she would shyly brush the side tendrils away from her face from time to time. Lily got an invitation from one of her friends to attend the ladies' conference that our mission team was organizing for her community. Lily was the product of a dysfunctional home; her father was an alcoholic and verbally and physically abused her mom and her siblings for years. She said her mother endured the almost daily beatings and berating from her father "for us, her kids."

She then told me in detail the horror of being the oldest child and not being able to protect her mother from her father. She regretted not applying herself in school and always getting below-average grades that disappointed her mother. Then Lily dropped a bombshell shocker. She was basically working as a prostitute, roaming the streets of Zimbabwe at night to sell her body. I took her hands in mine and asked her why she would do this. Her answer was short. She said with a flat affect: "Because I hate my father."

I found out that Lily was a victim of incest and rape at the hands of her father for several years. She had lost her innocence, her youth, and her virginity to the very man who was supposed to protect her. The emotional toll was so deep in Lily's heart that she had contemplated suicide and had even formulated a plan to carry it out.

She decided to attend the conference even though she was unsure of what to expect. Lily encountered something in the conference that was even more powerful than all the hatred and rage she had in her heart. She had a radical encounter with Jesus and surrendered her life to Him. As we talked, she asked me how she was supposed to feel about her father.

I explained the process of healing and forgiving her father. She had a physical reaction when I mentioned the word *forgiveness*. "I can't," she said. "He has to pay for what he did." I prayed and cried with Lily. I tried to help her understand what true forgiveness looked like and how Jesus forgives her, even when she does not deserve it. Lily sobbed throughout the rest of the conversation. I told her that God is just and that one day her father would stand before God to give an account of his life, just as she would. We exchanged contact information, and I told Lily to keep me informed of what was going on in her life via Facebook and social media.

I returned home and have continued to pray for Lily, that God would heal her and give her the grace to remove offense from her heart. I also pray for all the Lilys out there whose hearts have been broken by those they love and trust. It is shocking how prevalent abuse and incest are in our society and how the selfishness of a few impacts thousands.

Abuse tends to be generational, moving from one family to the next, from one family line to the next. You may think you deserve to feel offended or that you have a right to harbor offense against someone. Joyce Meyer says it this way: "We must learn to look at what people have done to themselves rather than what they have done to us. Usually, when someone hurts another, he or she has probably damaged him- or herself at least as much and is probably suffering some fall-out as a result."[2] Offense will always test our surrender to God.

STAY PLANTED

Can you pass the test of offense, or will it ruin the glorious work that God wants to do in your life because of the difficulty you're walking through? Offense comes because we have high expectations of people in our lives, even higher of people close to us, even higher still for other Christians, and highest still for God!

Sometimes we allow people to offend us, and we never let our seed of faith grow. Especially when it comes to church life, there will always be plenty of opportunities to be offended; you must choose to stay planted in the local church. Psalm 92:13 says, "Those who are planted in the house of the LORD shall flourish in the courts of our God" (NKJV). I love the word *thrive*, which is defined as "to grow vigorously: flourish; to gain in wealth or possessions: prosper; to progress toward or realize a goal."[3] If our goal is to flourish, prosper, or grow vigorously, then we must thrive where God has planted us.

When we work so closely with people, there will be

chances for misunderstandings to take place, for feelings to be hurt, and for sparks to fly. The fact that there is conflict is not the problem; the way we handle the conflict makes the difference. The local church is the hope of the world and is God's plan A to bring love and hope to our world. God is asking us to partner with Him in building the only thing that God is building, as it says in Matthew 16:18: "And I tell you that you are Peter, and on this rock I will build my church, and the gates of Hades will not overcome it." If the gates of hell can't even prevail against the church, why should offense?

God has anointed us to be *the* church in the earth, His church, a prevailing, powerful force on the earth. You can't be offended and anointed at the same time; you must choose one or the other. Let's not over-spiritualize this issue. Offense is a choice, just as surrender is a choice.

Planting speaks to commitment and sacrifice. If you have ever tried to plant anything, then you know this: it takes patience and tender, loving care to get a plant to grow. Even the sturdiest of plants needs a dedicated and faithful owner who will make sure it has enough water, sun, etc., to grow. When we plant the seed of our potential in the thriving, healthy soil of the local church, we will see how much fruit can come out of our lives. There is no way to anticipate the potential of fruit contained in a seed until you plant it.

The local church is the catalyst for that growth; it places the right amount of strain and pressure on the seed to allow what is inside that seed to be germinated. In my life, planting myself in my church has meant that I make choices based on the fact that I have been planted in the house of God. I will not uproot myself from the house until God tells me to, because a seed that keeps being transplanted from one place to another will eventually stop having fruit and die an untimely death. It doesn't matter if the seed is supposed to grow into a mighty, majestic oak; if it's never given the right soil in which to grow and *stay* rooted and planted in that soil, it will not fulfill its destiny to become a mighty oak.

Surrender means to die like a seed in the ground because that is the only way to discover your true potential and destiny. I don't serve in God's house so I can be noticed or rewarded; I serve because I love God, and I owe a debt I will never be able to repay. It is my greatest honor and privilege to serve God, and even if He never did another thing for me, I would still serve Him all the days of my life. If you serve with ulterior motives, you are opening yourself up for offense. To play a part in building the church of Jesus Christ is greater than any individual part we play.

I have heard it said this way, "The goal is greater than the role." I realize in serving in the house of God that I am building something under whose shade I may never sit—and that's OK. The fact that I get to be a part of something God is building is reward enough for me.

Maybe you have been hurt by a church in the past. Perhaps what is coming to mind now is the moral failure of a leader or the betrayal of a friend you trusted. I pray that right now you will receive healing in this area. Even when people aren't good, God is still good. Let us never confuse the two. Our job is not to judge others; God is the best judge. Our job is to be faithful to where God has called

> Surrender means to die like a seed in the ground because that is the only way to discover your true potential and destiny.

us, to love God, and to love others. If we hold on to our right to be hurt and offended, we will never fully enjoy the abundant life God promised to us.

KISS IT GOOD-BYE

Another area that can open us up for offense is when we are waiting on God for something. I will be the first to admit that I don't like to wait. I always look for the shortest checkout line at the grocery store, the fastest way to exit a building, and the quickest recipes to cook. Patience, or the lack thereof, is almost universal. Many meals that our parents or grandparents cooked took an hour or more. We can heat up the same thing in the microwave in six and a half minutes. We don't like to wait, because good things come to those who push buttons.

"Are we there yet?" Since the dawn of time, this familiar line has greeted parents from the backseats of cars, buggies, camels, and rickshaws. Across the millennia, only minutes after pulling out of the driveway, children have begun the familiar dialogue with their parents. *"Are we there yet? No. Are we there yet? No. Now? No. Soon? Yes. Are we there yet? No. We are not there yet! We have a long way to go!"* Kids will always ask whether they've reached their destination.

Adults know that the trip will be long, but we know where we're going, we have a sense of the distance, and we have a picture of the goal. For the sake of illustration, if we are the children, then God is the one driving with the map in His hands. We have to resist the temptation to take over the control of the direction of where God is taking us. We have a tendency to take matters into our own hands when we are waiting for God to come through. The truth is that God can do more in our waiting than we can do in our doing.

The story of Abraham and Sarah intrigues me. God gave them this incredible promise of a child, and Sarah gets offended as she waits on God. Sarah tries to play God and takes matters into her own hands—and into her bedroom. Before we judge Sarah too harshly, though, don't we do the same thing when we expect God to come through for us, at the time we want, in the way we want, and how we want? Let's settle this issue; when you're waiting on God for something, know that God loves you and He has the best in mind for you.

Whether God chooses to do something is a question of His sovereignty, not a question of His ability or His compassion for you. If you have been praying for something and it looks like nothing is happening, don't worry, because God is moving on your behalf—even now! Sometimes growing looks like waiting. As you're waiting, it may look like nothing is happening, but something supernatural is happening.

As you're waiting, you're growing, because God knows you need a depth in your relationship with Him that goes beyond emotion. Don't try to fix a God-sized problem with a man-sized answer, it just doesn't fit! We need to be mature enough in our faith to withstand unanswered prayers and the pressures of life; we need our roots to go down deep.

Our life journey with God can be a long, arduous one with obstacles, where, like children, we engage God in the all-too-familiar dialogue: *"Are we there yet? No. I asked You to help me with my addiction; are we there yet? No. I need help making that big decision; are we there yet?*

Soon. *I'm ready for my relationship to be fixed; are we there yet?* No. *Now?* No. *Soon?* Yes. *Now?* No. Please be patient. We have just a little longer to go." Patience is a fruit of the Spirit, so allow the Holy Spirit, not your impatience, to guide your life.

ABBY'S STORY

I have a friend we'll call Abby. I met her when we were both single, and we immediately bonded and enjoyed a close friendship. We were both passionate about our relationships with God, and we served faithfully at the churches we were planted in. At work we would chat about everything from what was on sale at the farmer's market that weekend to serious subjects such as our life's purpose.

Since Abby was a few years older than me, she definitely felt a strong desire to get married and start having children. As the years passed, the desire turned to pressure and then desperation. It didn't help that people would sometimes view her singleness as a problem to be solved, a puzzle to be completed, or worse yet, like a disease to be cured: "Oh, you're still single. I've got something for that. My cousin has this friend you just have to meet."

Well-meaning people would try to set her up on blind dates or give her tips on strategies to make herself more attractive and accessible to single guys. I also noticed that her criteria for the man she was looking for started getting shorter and less detailed.

Abby really started to hone in on this one issue. It slowly began to be the only thing she talked about or focused on. She viewed any social activity as a potential date waiting to happen, and any single, Christian man in our age range was fair game for Abby. When I started dating my husband, Abby was still single, and I could sense some distance creep into our relationship. She was not as eager to celebrate with me when I got engaged as I thought she would be.

After a period of a few months of not hearing from Abby, I tracked her down through some mutual friends. I then found out that she was expecting a baby, and the father of her child was not in her life. I called Abby, and we cried together on the phone. She regretted her compromise and wished she had waited on God. I encouraged her as much as I could, telling her that the gifts of God in her life were without repentance and we can't sin so much that God's grace can't cover us.

Abby could have just given up and settled in to a life of being a single mother. Instead she chose to forgive herself and kiss her mistake good-bye. She enrolled in school, finished college, and today is back in ministry. She made a purposeful, conscious decision to let go of her past and walk boldly into the future that God has for her. Before she could do this, she had to surrender her mistake to God, ask for forgiveness, and then let it go.

> Once you surrender your life to God, you have to let go of your past.

Steps one and two of this process are relatively easy, but the "letting go" can prove to be difficult. If you find yourself in a similar place that Abby was, let today be the day that you let it go. The best is yet to come in your life. In Christ we can let go of our past and walk in the newness of our identity in Christ. Past experiences don't define you. Maybe someone in your past said you would never amount to anything and you believed it. Or maybe you weren't great academically, so you just believe, "I'm average. I made average grades. I'm average, so I'm going to have an average life."

Perhaps you had the dream of a great marriage, and as much as you wanted a great marriage, one day you ended up divorced. And now you feel like you go through life with this big D on your forehead that says you failed because you couldn't hold your marriage together. You're not that good of a Christian. You've been divorced.

You may have felt the sting of rejection if someone said to you, "You'd be so much prettier if you lost ten pounds," and so you just went on a downward spiral through insecurity and self-doubt.

Once you surrender your life to God, you have to let go of your past. You are not who others say you are, you are not what happened to you in the past, and you are not the sum total of your past experiences. You are who God says you are.

Chapter Nine

LOSING CONTROL

If anyone would come after me, he must deny him-self and take up his cross daily and follow me. For whoever wants to save his life will lose it, but whoever loses his life for me will save it.
—JESUS CHRIST, IN LUKE 9:23–24

HI. MY NAME is Mercy, and I am a control freak. There, I said it. I would not so readily admit it if I didn't know it was true, but it is. It started way back in my youth. I remember getting sweaty palms in class when the teacher mentioned "group paper." I would be the first to volunteer to do the conclusion of the group paper because that meant I could see what everyone already contributed to the paper and change it if needed before it got turned in for an assignment. I could not imagine being the one doing the introduction and not knowing what the finished product would be before we turned it in to the teacher.

I like things done a certain way. I always clean my house starting with the kitchen first, and I do the bathrooms last. OK, perhaps I am a little obsessive about the cleanliness of my house. I have a system for everything: planning, cooking, organizing, and even working out. As a mother, I relish the fact that I can plan my children's day out for them, and I am always a step ahead in anticipating what their needs will be. I am the proverbial backseat driver who pumps the imaginary brake when I'm not in the driver's seat. I can't stand seeing indicators on my phone for missed phone calls, voice mails, or text messages. I clear them out as soon as they appear so I don't keep thinking I have a task I have not yet completed. At any given time I have a constant to-do list in my head with little imaginary checkmarks when I complete a task. So I think we've settled the fact that I have a few issues with being in control.

The only problem with being a control freak is that you can't categorize what you feel the need to control. It usually doesn't just stop at cleaning or organizing; it extends way beyond that to the deep recesses of your soul. It has a way of bleeding over into every area of your life, and all of a sudden you can't feel the subtle promptings to change, to shift, or to go in a different direction. Many times this is exactly what is needed for growth. Our surrender to God requires us to grow in areas, and in order to do that we have to lose control of our lives. As long as I hold tight on to the reins of my life, I can never go on the epic adventure God wants to take me on.

I'VE GOT ME ON THE BRAIN

I could hardly see through my tears. My husband had just told me we might have to move. I started imagining packing up my life in boxes, pulling my child out of school, leaving my church family, and starting all over. I thought of all the years we had sowed and planted into our lives here. There are some things that can only be reaped through longevity and faithfulness. I thought of all the worst possible scenarios and dwelt on them. I just did not want to do it. I was comfortable here, we were surrounded by our friends, we loved our church family…and I didn't want to move.

Now, as a wife, I knew the decision was not solely mine to make, but that made me even more anxious. My husband loves me and values my input, but at the end of the day the decision had to be made between him and God. I had to take myself, and my crazy emotional rants, out of the picture and allow my husband to seek the Lord and make a decision that was good for our entire family.

> Our surrender to God requires us to grow in areas, and in order to do that we have to lose control of our lives.

Let me tell you, nothing tests your surrender to God like when you have to submit to a decision you don't necessarily agree with. The prospect of it tests your heart; it reveals the true state of your decision to surrender to God. That passage, Luke 9:23–24, tells me that *every single day* I need to deny myself and take up my cross to follow Jesus. Daily—every fresh twenty-four hours—I need to reaffirm my commitment to surrender to God and lose control of my life. I battled with this prospect of change; I preemptively mourned the loss of all the ways my life would change, though I hadn't lost a single thing. The pain of having to think about leaving people I had "done life" with for ten years was too much to bear. It was like I was grieving for something I had not yet lost.

I said one thing, but my heart felt another. I said I was willing to go wherever God would send me, but my heart was holding on with white knuckles to the life we had. My mouth had sung all the right songs about surrendering all to God—going where He leads, moving when He moves, following where He leads—but my heart was not willing to follow through on the promise my mouth made. It's so important when we face change to make sure we are operating from a place of Spirit-led wisdom rather than emotional upheaval.

Jeremiah 17:9 says, "The heart is deceitful above all things and beyond cure. Who can understand it?" We were not made to follow our hearts. God tells us to guard our hearts in Proverbs 4:23. Not only should we guard our hearts, but we should also follow the Spirit in Romans 8:6, which says, "The mind controlled by the Spirit is life and peace." Don't follow the emotions of your heart. Guard your heart and follow the Holy Spirit's promptings and guidance.

I had to resolve in my heart that I am willing to go wherever God sends me. As long as His presence is with me, I will go. I would follow my husband to the ends of the earth if God led us there. This is so much easier to type than to do and truly mean it. As difficult and painful as the process was, it helped my husband and me grow closer to God and each other. I am in covenant with my husband, not with a geographic location, and I willingly surrender my will to God and submit myself to my husband. I love that man with everything in me, and I would follow him to the ends of the earth, God with us.

If you like to be in control, you need to know something that I've learned: you are not the main character, and it's not your show to run. Believe it or not, the world does not revolve around you, and things will not fall apart if you're not in control. God is in control, and trust me, that's the way we want it to be. Many of us think we don't like change, but really we just don't like losing control.

There were many days when I would lock myself in our closet and just lie on the floor and weep, crying out to God because I knew He was showing me the condition of my heart, and it was not pretty. The truth was, I liked the comfort of my life, and I didn't want to change. There are times when comfort can be just as dangerous as sin. Worse yet, I was just being self-centered instead of others-focused. It was easy for Jesus to resign control of His life to God because He was focused on other people. If we cut your heart, would you bleed others, or would it be your comfort, your blessings, and yourself that flowed out?

All Cracked Up

I could see them creeping up the side of the wall, a spidery network of cracks. We simply patched them up, put a fresh coat of paint and didn't think about them again. That is until they resurfaced two weeks later. The same patchwork routine happened as well as the fresh coat of paint. Needless to say, I was very frustrated when a few weeks later those pesky cracks showed up again on the same wall.

At this point, we decided that we needed to hire a professional to take a look at the walls. After he came out and inspected everything, he said, "Ma'am, you don't have a crack problem."

"Oh really," I thought, as I stood there impatiently with my arms folded across my chest, staring at the crack problem this man was saying I did not have.

"Your real problem is not the cracks on the wall; that's just a symptom of a deeper issue. You don't have a crack problem; you have a foundation problem. The main issue is the foundation of the house."

The man went on to explain that the cracks were simply a manifestation of the fact that the foundation of the house was shifting ever slightly, and thus the walls were shifting as well, creating the cracks.

I couldn't help but think that perhaps the things God allows to happen to us are not the real problem; the problem is what those things reveal in our hearts. The best way to navigate disappointment and trials is to examine what they expose. If I had never been presented with the idea of moving, perhaps I would not have seen my heart for what it was. The doubt, fear, and insecurity that rose to the surface had always been there, festering beneath the surface. The adverse situation just revealed it.

The Bible tells us the story of two men who are building a house in Matthew 7:24–27. Those men had much in common. They were both building a house. They both had access to hear the Word of God, and they both probably were anticipating a positive future. The similarities cease when you introduce one thing: the storm. Once the storm came, one man was called foolish and the other was called wise. Jesus said the wise one heard the word of the Lord and did what it said. The foolish man heard the word of the Lord and did not do it. Wisdom then is not found in how much you know, but in what you do with what you know. The wise person is not the one who has the most knowledge, but the one who makes the best choices using what he knows.

If you are seeing cracks on the wall of your heart, emotions that are unhealthy, excesses that are out of control, or decisions that aren't wise, don't focus on the cracks. Dig deeper and look at the foundation. What kind

> The best way to navigate disappointment and trials is to examine what they expose.

of foundation are you building on? Until your foundation is built on the rock that is Jesus, you will always be doing patchwork in your life. True surrender to God looks like applying the wisdom found in the Bible no matter what life is throwing your way. There is no doubt that the storms will come. Life happens. People get sick, financial distress occurs, children decide to behave in a wayward manner, friends disappoint us, and prayers do not get answered in the manner we would like. When these things happen, don't rage against God; look inside your heart and choose to trust God. When the contrary winds of gale force rock your world, don't resist it. Allow it to reveal what you're made of and how you've been built.

LET IT GO

Most of us do not want to relinquish control of our lives because we are afraid of what God will ask us to give up if we really give our lives to Him and truly surrender. Maybe you are waiting for some future event, some better time or a perfect set of circumstances before you will surrender to God. If you have read this book up to this point, then you must desire to truly surrender to God. But if you don't lose control of your life, it's not true surrender.

I am always challenged by the majestic language of this prayer penned by the early Puritans. It's entitled "Man a Nothing" and is written anonymously; it must be a brave soul who would own up to these words.

> When thou wouldst guide me I control myself, when thou wouldst be sovereign I rule myself. When thou wouldst take care of me I suffice myself. When I should depend on thy providings I supply myself, when I should submit to thy providence I follow my will. When I should study, love, honour, trust thee, I serve myself; I fault and correct thy laws to suit myself, instead of thee I look to man's approbation, and am by nature an idolater. Lord, it is my chief design to bring my heart back to thee. Convince me that I cannot be my own god, or make myself happy, nor my own Christ to restore my joy, nor my own Spirit to teach, guide, rule me. Take away my roving eye, curious ear, greedy appetite, lustful heart; show

me that none of these things can heal a wounded
conscience, or support a tottering frame, or uphold
a departing spirit. Then take me to the cross and
leave me there.[1]

The cross is the ultimate expression of losing control and
letting go. Philippians tells us that Jesus "did not regard
equality with God a thing to be grasped" (Phil 2:6, NAS).
At the cross He let it go, lost it all, and emptied Himself.
In so doing, He fulfilled His destiny! Always needing to be
in control of your life is like settling for less than your full
potential. God has a grand and wonderful scheme for your
life, but it will never happen if you don't let Him propel
you.

This year my family and I watched the neighborhood
Fourth of July celebrations, including the fireworks. I love
explosives and pyrotechnics of any kind: rockets, sparklers,
and bangers, I like them all. I am always amazed at how
some firecrackers are wrapped in nondescript, boring
brown paper. Some of the sparklers are gray, muted,
unattractive, and unimpressive—at first. They only stay
that way when they are encased in their wrapping, but
once they leave the control of their outer casing and are
launched into the sky, they burst into a panorama of colors.

It fills me with childlike awe to watch the circles of
colors trace the sky; something about the vibrant points
of light against the backdrop of a dark sky is breathtaking.
Indeed, those gathered around to watch the fireworks
always gasp in admiration and enjoyment. How can
something so small and unimpressive create the majestic
displays in the sky for all to see? It had to leave its casing,
what it was wrapped in, and then be launched into the

sky. This is exactly what God wants to do with our lives. Right now we are wrapped in the common brown paper of flesh, but if we surrender what we are to Him and give up our control, He can unveil something far more beautiful and majestic in us than we could ever imagine. Surrender reveals surprises God has in store for you; don't let it wait another moment. Let. It. Go.

God is always at work to make us more like Jesus, and everything that comes into our lives—good or bad—He uses for that purpose. God's aim for your life is not just to make you happy, rich, or famous; it's to make you more like Jesus.

YOUR EPIC LIFE

Has God allowed conflict or disappointment in your life? Think about this for a moment: perhaps God has allowed this as part of the process for you to lose control of your life and become a part of the great epic He is writing with your life. I love epic movies, especially romantic ones. Something resonates in me when I see Prince Charming slip that glass slipper on Cinderella's foot, or when Rose is standing at the bow of the *Titanic* with Jack holding her— or even in real life, when Prince William kissed Kate on that balcony at Buckingham Palace. You see, the characters in these stories all had to overcome some disappointment and conflict before they emerged as someone great.

Jeff Goins puts it this way in his blog post "When Life Doesn't Turn Out the Way You Want." Jeff says:

> Every character in a story wants something. But she doesn't always get it. At least, not how she anticipated or planned. That's the difference

between *Friends* and *Lord of the Rings*. One is all about each character's petty melodrama. Another is an epic. No offense to Joey, Ross, Phoebe and the rest of the gang (because I love them dearly), but which would you rather live? Having your plans wrecked is an essential element to living a significant story and being an interesting character.[2]

The epic that God is weaving with the storylines of our lives is one to stand in awe of. This story started in the Garden of Eden; contained in the redemption and deliverance of the Jews are the seeds of our own redemption. In the blood of the lamb painted over the doorposts of the houses in the first Passover, we see the blood of our Lamb, Jesus. His blood is painted over us, turning away judgment and saving us by grace. We can see our history all through the Old Testament and crossing over into the new covenant. Jesus is the central theme of this epic, and we can find ourselves in the pages of every story in the Bible.

John Eldredge says it beautifully: "For when we were born, we were born into the midst of a great story begun before the dawn of time. A story of adventure, of risk and loss, heroism...and betrayal. A story where good is warring against evil, danger lurks around every corner, and glorious deeds wait to be done.... There is a larger story and you have a crucial role to play."[3]

The problem is that we don't understand the story fully, and sometimes it feels as if we skipped a few pages of our story or lost focus on what kind of story our lives should become. Ecclesiastes 3:11 says, "He has also set eternity in

the hearts of men; yet they cannot fathom what God has
done from beginning to end."

Love in Disguise

There are parts of the story God is telling with our lives that
we will not fully understand. Sometimes disappointment
uncovers your destiny, and your pain can reveal great
purpose. Take my life as an example. The trial I endured
with losing my mother and brother produced the testimony
in the book you are reading right now. I have had the great
privilege of preaching and teaching all over the world to
thousands of people, and this same story is proclaimed.

Truthfully there are times, however, when love comes
in disguised in a trial, disappointment, or difficult times.
Think about all the love stories you watched as a child such
as *Beauty and the Beast*. Beneath the unpleasant exterior
of the beast was a handsome prince. Or even the epic movie
I referenced at the beginning of this book, *The Princess
Bride*. The farmhand was exactly what the princess desired
all along; he just did not look like what she expected. God
is telling a love story with our lives, and we know that we
will have a happy ending, but sometimes God's love does
not look like what we expect or think it should.

Life sometimes causes us to lose our grip on God's love,
and our pain causes us to doubt not only God's power and
ability, but worse, to also doubt His love for us. Maybe
right now you're thinking, "I'm no Cinderella, and the glass
slipper is not fitting. My life is far from epic. It's reality
and it's hard." If you feel as if your life is out of control,
that may be the greatest motivator for you to trust God.
Your greatest disappointment, trial, or delay may simply
be God's love in disguise. When the unexpected happens,

expect God to show up because God's grace is sometimes best seen in the face of suffering.

The familiar story of Lazarus in John 11:1–3 illustrates this idea of how disappointment builds our character and love sometimes comes in disguise. Lazarus and his sisters, Mary and Martha, knew and loved Jesus. This was the same Mary who had massaged Jesus's feet and wiped them with her hair. This shows the level of familiarity and intimacy this family had with Jesus.

It would make sense, then, that when someone in the family became sick, the sisters would send word to Jesus, and they did in John 11:3: "Lord, the one you *love* is sick" (emphasis added). The sisters appealed to Jesus's love, not His power, deity, or ability, but His love for them. Have you ever done that? Approached Jesus on the basis of His love for you and then based His answer on that same scale?

Curiously, when Jesus received their message, the Bible says He stayed where He was for two more days.

> Your greatest disappointment, trial, or delay may simply be God's love in disguise.

My first instinct is to wonder why Jesus did not rush to Lazarus's side and intervene before anything bad happened, since He loved Lazarus. Jesus's love was not in question, *yet* when He heard that Lazarus was sick, He stayed where He was for two more days. I bet if you think back over your life, you have had a few moments when God did not make any sense. "God, if You really love me, then why did my mother die?" "Why will You not help me get over this addiction, if You love me?" "Why am I still struggling financially?" "God, I thought You loved me."

Let's be honest; this is Jesus we're talking about—the

same God who spoke the world into existence and formed us out of dust. He could wave a hand and still waves, shut the mouths of lions, and raise people from the dead. Healing a friend does not seem like it would put a great demand on Jesus. Yet the Bible is very clear about the fact that *because* of that love, not *in spite* of it, there was a delay in Lazarus's healing. God's delays have a divine purpose. If God has delayed something in your life or if things did not turn out the way you wanted them to, perhaps it's because your story is larger than you think. You are part of something bigger than yourself.

There is no way for us to fully grasp the entire scope of the story our lives will tell. Lazarus had no idea what the scope of his story would be, but we do know that Lazarus's story was not just about him. It was about other people. How do I know this? The Bible states it very clearly in John 11:14–15. Jesus is speaking to the disciples and says this: "Lazarus is dead, and for your sake I am glad I was not there, so that you may believe."

Wow, did Jesus just say what I think He said? Those letters are in red in my Bible, so they came straight from the mouth of our Lord and Savior. He said it was for the sake of the disciples He was glad that Lazarus, whom He loved, was dead! I thought this was Lazarus's story, so when did it become about the disciples? The story is larger than Lazarus or his sisters can imagine.

Is it possible that your trial, your disappointment, your delay, your pain, does not end with you? If you surrender your life to Jesus, can your suffering actually give someone else new grounds to believe and an opportunity to increase their faith in God? I dare to say yes to that. As a matter of fact, the book you are holding in your hands right now is a result of that very process in my life. God wanted to involve a few more people on the way to giving Lazarus his healing. I wonder who is in your path on your delay, on the story God is telling with your life, who needs to have their faith built up?

FOURTH-DAY MIRACLE

When Jesus finally got to Lazarus, he had already been in the tomb for four days. The Jews believed the soul, or the spirit, of a person who had died lingered over the corpse for three days, then the spirit abandoned the body because any hope of resuscitation was gone. Jesus arrived on the fourth day, the day that was beyond all hope. All through Scripture the third day is the day when God acts. Jesus arrived on the hopeless day, the fourth. By this time the disciples were involved in the story, but here came Martha, the older sister. She went out to meet Jesus, and she was a verifiable control freak.

I can relate to Martha, as I'm both an older and a younger sibling, and as I already mentioned, I like to be gripping the steering wheel and moving the bus. There's a reason older sisters came out first; we keep everyone else in line. It's the older-sister syndrome—pray for us!

Remember this story started out with Lazarus needing a miracle from Jesus, but as his miracle was being delayed, Jesus had something for Martha. I can almost hear the disappointment in her voice: "'Lord,'" Martha said to Jesus, 'if you had been here, my brother would not have died'" (John 11:21). And then she tried to do some damage control and quickly added, "But I know that even now God will give you whatever you ask" (v. 22).

Martha reminds me of a lot of Christians who feel that

God has let them down but are still trying to put up a façade of faith. We know all the right things to say; we know the right things to post on Twitter and Facebook. We know how to keep up a good appearance on the outside, uphold a façade and look the part. If we are honest, though, on the inside we are falling apart. After my mom died, I almost didn't know how to interact with other Christians. I felt embarrassed, I didn't want them to pity me, so I put on a brave face. I even did this with God for a while. I still went to church, raised my hands at the right times, and pretended I had faith.

Martha tried to do this with Jesus, but He cut right through her pretense and got right to the heart of the issue with these four words: "Do you believe this?" (v. 26). Jesus was not asking about belief that is an intellectual assent, but rather He questioned the condition of her heart. Do you believe?

Sometimes when we are waiting for God to come through for us, we believe God *can* do what we have asked, but we don't believe that He *will* do it for us. Jesus was saying, "Martha, I know we're close. I know we hang out. I know you worship Me. I know you serve Me. You've set a table for Me, but *do you believe?* I know you sing it, I know you preach it, I know you amen it, but when your believing is tested, *do you believe?*"

God is asking you: *If you believe, then why have you stopped asking for healing? If you believe I can come through for you, then why have you given up hope? If you believe that when you sow you reap, then why have you cut back on your giving? Do you believe the plans I have for you, and if so, why have you stopped dreaming big? Why have all your dreams come true because you dreamed too little?* Perhaps, like me, God wants to use you, in your situation, to help with someone else's unbelief.

TRUTH AND TEARS

Lazarus's story did not end with the disciples and Martha. There was also the emotional wreck of a younger sister, Mary. We find her at Jesus's feet, the same feet she had sat at to learn, the same feet she had bathed and wiped with her hair. She told Jesus the *exact* same thing her older sister had said, but His reaction was very different.

Jesus's response to Martha was to confront her with truth. He knew she had control issues, and His response was strong to show her who was really in control. Mary's issue was not unbelief; it was a broken heart, so His response to Mary was to comfort her with tears. He was speechless, and for the first recorded time in the Bible Jesus wept. I wonder who is brokenhearted on your journey that you are supposed to be reaching out to. Your difficulty is not meant to turn you inward; it's meant to turn you outward to think of others. God wants to use you to heal the brokenhearted.

At this point, a crowd had formed, and Lazarus's story expanded to include all of these people. John 11:37 says: "But some of them said, 'Could not he who opened the eyes of the blind man have kept this man from dying?'" Some in the crowd were not doubting His power or His ability; they knew Jesus could heal, but they were doubting His love!

Their doubts were about to be silenced, though, by the miracle Jesus was about to perform. As a result of Lazarus's delayed miracle, many in that crowd would see the miracle Jesus performed and put their faith in Him. What started out as a death became life and salvation for many more than just Lazarus. Your delay, your roundabout journey, your love in disguise, may be an occasion to silence the doubt in someone else's heart.

But before Jesus can go further, here came Martha, the control freak, again. She couldn't quite let it go, and she said this: "But Lord...by this time there is a bad odor, for he has been there four days" (John 11:39). I can't help but chuckle to myself because I can really sympathize with Martha. I would be one to bust out some potpourri or Yankee Candles to handle the stench, as well. Jesus looked her full in the face, probably even eye to eye, and said, "Did I not tell you that if you believed, you would see the glory of God?" (v. 40). He was telling Martha, "The story is larger than you think, and you have a crucial role to play."

Think about this. The raising of Lazarus convinced Israel's religious leaders that they had to take more drastic action to kill Jesus. Jesus's decision to raise Lazarus directly led to His arrest and crucifixion.

Jesus knew this, and yet He did it anyway. He knew that as soon as He called Lazarus forth He would have to endure the cross for you and me. Lazarus's miracle was not just about him; it was about the disciples to strengthen their faith, it was about Martha to help her unbelief, it was about Mary to heal her broken heart, it was about the critics to silence their doubt, and it was about you and me—to give us everlasting life in the revealing of epic love.

What an epic is Lazarus's story—and our story is just as dramatic and impactful. You need to know that when you lose control of your life, God will take over and write an incredible epic with what you've given Him. If God has allowed change, conflict, or disappointments to enter your life, know that He will make it a testimony one day. God is writing an epic tale with your life. Once upon eternity your story will have a happy ending. A mighty King who loves you with an everlasting love will return at the sound of the trumpet, the clouds will roll back like a scroll, and He will come riding in on a white horse looking for His bride. God has given us faith for the past in the finished work of Jesus, hope for the future, and love for the present.

Chapter Ten

LOOK BOTH WAYS

*From the [example of] the past, the man of the present
acts prudently so as not to imperil the future.*[1]
—TITIAN, EIGHTEENTH-CENTURY VENETIAN ARTIST

W E WERE SITTING on our front porch watching a spectacular sunset. The vivid hues of pinks, oranges, and blues were absolutely gorgeous. My son and I sat and watched the sun slowly become concealed by a veil of wispy, thin clouds. We sat appreciating the beauty of it all silently for a few minutes. Then Isaiah turned to me and said, "Mom, I wish I could just wrap the sky up in a bow and give it to you as a gift." The generosity of heart and love that my child displayed melted my heart, and if my son had asked for our house or our car or anything else right then and there, it would have been his!

Every day I spend with my children is leaving a mark on them. I am living and leaving my legacy all at the same time. Your legacy is not something you leave once you die; it's the life you are living right now. When I decide to sacrifice sleep to wake up early to pray for my husband and children, I am living my legacy. When I use discipline as a teachable moment rather than to vent on my child, I am living my legacy. Little eyes and ears are watching and hearing all I do or say. I am living and leaving my legacy. When I look at my children, I am convinced more than ever of the necessity for my life to make a difference. I feel a weight to raise God-fearing, world-changing children who will put God first every day of their lives.

Perhaps the best example of a surrendered mother who understood the power of her legacy is Hannah (1 Sam. 1). She was the wife of Elkanah and struggled with infertility and depression. Elkanah had a second wife, Peninah, who had children and made life miserable for

> Your legacy is not something you leave once you die; it's the life you are living right now.

Hannah. In those days for a woman to be childless was not just a handicap, but it was also seen as a curse from God. Year after year Hannah would make her way to the temple to pray. On one occasion she prayed with such fervor that the priest thought she was drunk!

First Samuel 1:11–18 says:

> Then she pulled herself together, slipped away quietly, and entered the sanctuary. The priest Eli was on duty at the entrance to GOD's Temple in the customary seat. Crushed in soul, Hannah prayed to GOD and cried and cried—inconsolably. Then she made a vow: Oh, GOD-of-the-Angel-Armies, if you'll take a good, hard look at my pain, if you'll quit neglecting me and go into action for me by giving me a son, I'll give him completely, unreservedly to you. I'll set him apart for a life of holy discipline.
>
> —THE MESSAGE

Completely and *unreservedly*: those are words that surrendered people use. God did answer Hannah, and He gave her a son, Samuel. After all Hannah had been through, it would seem that what would be best for Hannah would be to keep her child; after all, he was vindication of her worth, proof that she was not cursed by God. But Hannah had already made a decision to surrender to God; she simply had to manage that decision when she was put to the test.

Hannah had the wisdom to realize that the purpose of having a child is not just for the joy of motherhood; it's to raise up the next generation to serve God. She wanted her son to dedicate himself to God, not just by profession but also by conviction. Children are not given to us just to manage; we have been charged by God to raise them up to be like arrows in the hand of a warrior, a supernatural gift from God to accomplish His purpose on the earth. Hannah understood this so deeply that it gave her courage to follow through on her vow to God.

Living With the Future in Mind

Do you have the same courage to give up that which you love the most in surrender to God without a guarantee? Are you willing to put a knife to the throat of your dream, your hope, or your desire with no guarantee of a ram in the thicket? Is your surrender complete and unreserved, or are you holding something back? Let us not hold the blessings of God so tightly that we are not willing to let them go if He asks us to. We have to hold on to God tighter than we hold on to the blessings God gives us.

Your surrender to God is part of your legacy. You are right now living the legacy you will leave behind. Your legacy does not happen sometime in the future, when you're older, when you get married, when your kids leave the house, when you go to college, or when you enter ministry full time; it's happening right now. The words "one day when" can become an obstacle to accomplishing God's will for your life. Jesus's surrender had implications for billions upon billions who were yet to be. He had to think with future generations in mind. We must do the same.

When you think of paying the price of surrendering to God, think generationally. How will your walk with God today affect those yet to come? My mother's walk with God, her surrender to the will of God even till her last breath, profoundly affected me, my family, the thousands I speak to every year, and even you, as you read my words. This is a gripping reminder of the impact of true surrender. How do you need to walk *now* so you can achieve a legacy *then*? How will your relationship with God now affect others in the future?

When I have what I call "heated fellowship" with my husband, there are certain things I will not let come out of my mouth because I know that I am in a covenant relationship with him. When I am ninety years old, I want to be sitting on a porch, holding hands with my sweetheart, reminiscing on all the days gone by. Since I know what kind of marriage I want then, I manage my decision to stay married to my husband now. I don't have to decide every time we have a disagreement whether I will stay with my husband. I already did that at the altar when I uttered the words "I do." I have to live with the future in mind. If you don't live your legacy, nobody will. No one can live your life except for you.

ASSUME THE POSITION

One of my favorite things to do as a mom is play sports with my children. My son just giggles with glee when he gets his turn at bat in baseball or when we tackle each other in football or kick the soccer ball around our backyard. There is something about the unhindered joy in a child's laugh; you can't help but smile when you hear it. On this particular day we were playing baseball, and he decided to be the pitcher; I would be the hitter.

As I stood waiting for his pitch, he got upset and said, "Mommy, you can't just stand there. You have to be ready to hit the baseball." What my son was telling me to do was to assume a position that would signal to him that I was ready to hit the ball. I have to assume a certain position. The way I gripped the bat, the degree of angle my elbow needed to have, the direction my head and shoulders were turned to, and the wide stance of my legs, these would all signal to my son that I was ready to hit the ball. The opposite is also true: when my grip, stance, and positioning were not in place, the pitcher would not release the ball for me to make a play at it.

God wants to deposit some truths into our lives, but because of all the myths and lies we believe, we're not able to get them. Some of these come from our past; many of them come from our hearts. We have believed lies about surrender, and they are making us act like I did with my son, "just standing there," instead of getting ready for the ball God wants to pitch to us. John 8:32 says, "Then you will know the truth, and the truth will set you free." As we dispel some of the myths we hold about surrender, we position ourselves to get what God is trying to give to us.

In my life the biggest lie I believed was this: *I should value my independence above all else.* I truly prided myself on the fact that I was a strong woman who could provide for herself emotionally and financially without relying on anyone. I would look down on girls who threw themselves at men, desperate for attention. People would sometimes ask why I was still single, and I would say something like, "I'm just doing my own thing right now. I don't really have time to date and all that." What sounds like freedom and independence was really self-righteousness and pride. I worked hard to prove that no person, especially a man, could control what I thought about myself or how I acted.

Thinking about allowing God take control of my life

threatened my sense of independence. "If I give my life to Christ, I won't be free to do what I want." Have you ever heard anyone say that? They have bought in to the lie that society upholds that says we should value freedom above all else. The truth is, surrender does not threaten our freedom, and the two are not mutually exclusive.

The alternative to surrender is not complete freedom; it is slavery to something or someone else. Either you surrender to God and enjoy true freedom, or you reject surrender and become a slave to sin. We think obeying God is at odds with "doing our own thing," but the truth is, our two options in life are either to be obedient to God or to be a slave to sin. The urge to "do your own thing" is not fueled by independence; it's fueled by the power of sin.

> The best way to express your individuality is to surrender it to God and allow Him propel you into a destiny that is custom-made for you.

Think about Adam and Eve in the Garden of Eden. Every temptation since then involves our going our own way instead of God's way. When it comes to your relationships, will you date your way or God's way? What about how you treat people you don't like? Will you decide to do it your way or God's way?

Know this: God's call to surrender is an invitation, not an ultimatum. You have to choose. Surrender opens the door for revelation and restoration. Obedience is our love for God expressed, and we cannot separate the two. Obedience feeds upon itself and makes it easier. As you obey, you know God better, and as you know Him better, you trust Him more. As you trust Him more, it's easier to obey.

Myth Busters

When I discuss the issue of surrender, the number-one reason people tell me they struggle to surrender to God is that they think it will diminish their sense of uniqueness and individuality. But surrender to God does not mean you give up rational thinking or achieve mindless acquiescence to the whims of someone else. God would not waste the amazing mind He gave you. If anyone values our uniqueness, it's God!

> The alternative to surrender is not complete freedom; it is slavery to something or someone else.

Have you ever been in a public place such as an airport or a classroom and just looked around at people? It's amazing how beautiful and unique we all are. No two people are alike, no two fingerprints are alike…not even identical twins! God values uniqueness. The hairs on our heads are not only counted but also numbered as well. The best way to express your individuality is to surrender it to God and allow Him propel you into a destiny that is custom-made for you.

No one on the planet can reach the people you can reach, leave the impact you were created to leave, or do what you can do. You do not discover who you are by striving and searching for yourself but by simply surrendering to what you already hope is true. You are marvelous, created by God to do remarkable things in an incredible way; so act like it! There is a quote from Marianne Williamson that I love:

> Our deepest fear is not that we are inadequate.
> Our deepest fear is that we are powerful beyond
> measure.…We ask ourselves, Who am I to

be brilliant, gorgeous, talented, and fabulous?
Actually, who are you *not* to be? You are a child
of God. Your playing small doesn't serve the
world....We are all meant to shine, as children
do. We are born to make manifest the glory of
God that is within us....As we are liberated from
our own fear, our presence automatically liberates
others.[2]

Can you honestly fill in the following line, "I am great
because _____"? I am a little
girl from Nigeria who had big dreams and surrendered
her life to a big God, and I have seen Him extract nothing
short of greatness in my life. It's almost as if we need
permission to be fabulous. Well, God is giving you that
permission...starting now!

Whatever your surrender to God will ask you to sacrifice
always pales in comparison to the kind of person surrender
will cause you to become. Simply put, surrender unlocks
your destiny. There were many years in my life when I went
through life without a clear sense of direction or purpose.

The missing key in my life was not knowledge,
understanding, or even wisdom. I had the desire to know
what God's plans were for my life, but I basically lived
how I wanted to despite that desire. It wasn't until I truly
surrendered my life to God after my mom died that I
realized that surrendered people really are the ones God
uses. God chose Mary to be Jesus's mother, not because
she was the best, most beautiful, or most talented, but
because of her spirit of surrender.

Look at her response in Luke 1:38: "I am the Lord's
servant...may it be to me as you have said." Other versions
say, "Be it unto me according to your Word." There is

nothing more powerful in the hands of a supernatural God than a life that is surrendered to Him.

Another common thing I hear from people is that surrender to God sounds boring and mundane. Christians should be having the most fun on the planet because we know that we are in a win-win situation! Jesus says in John 10:10: "I have come that you may have *life*, and have it to the *full*" (emphasis added). I had to resist the urge to put exclamation points on the end of that sentence because nothing about that says boring, mundane, or sacrifice to me. It's not a riddle or a revelation; God actually wants us to be happy!

Most of us have tried what the world is offering to us to make us happy. I am both saddened and amazed as the lifestyles of the rich and famous take a downward spiral after reaching the pinnacle of success and fame. These Hollywood stars and starlets we emulate and idolize, multimillionaires who should not have a care in the world, struggle with depression, emptiness, and misery. We watch as beautiful people marry even more beautiful people, just for it to end in divorce and tragedy. We are all witnesses to the demise of once-popular singers as their lives end in death at the hands of dangerous vices such as drugs and alcohol. They make ego-dominated decisions and then lack the spiritual resources to cope with the aftermath of their decisions.

This is what the Bible calls "death" transmitted from family to family, generation to generation, from the Garden of Eden to the soil of our hearts today. Of course, we can experience momentary happiness and money can buy us fleeting joy, but it will never last until we surrender our lives to God. It seems there is an empty hunger on the inside of all of us that only God can fill. Surrender not only fills the God-void, but it also gives us the power and boldness to overcome our weakness and live the full life God has for us.[3]

Chapter Eleven

BOLD AND RECKLESS

My past is redeemed. My present makes sense. My future is secure. I'm done and finished with low living, sight walking, small planning, smooth knees, color-less dreams, tamed visions, mundane talking, cheap living, and dwarfed goals.... I don't have to be right, or first, or tops, or recognized, or praised, or rewarded. I live by faith, lean on His presence, walk by patience, lift by prayer, and labor by Holy Spirit power.
—AUTHOR UNKNOWN

T HE VIBRANT DECLARATION quoted above is part of a letter called "Fellowship of the Unashamed" attributed to a young pastor in Zimbabwe who was martyred for his faith. When you surrender your life to God, the result is a sense of mission. You're motivated to leave your past and walk boldly into the future. The truth is that we are all on a mission, whether we know it or not.

What is your mission? What are you living for? What do you exist for? When you wake up each day, what do you live to do? Some of us are on a mission to live the American dream: life, liberty, and the pursuit of happiness. We want to succeed in life and have fun doing it. Most of us would agree that we want a safe, comfortable life. The problem comes when we surrender our lives to God and He asks us to give up our safe, comfortable life for one of His making. What you once regarded as comfort has now become a distraction. To live a life that's worthy of the sacrifice you are making in surrender may require you to be brave, maybe even a bit reckless.

KATIE'S STORY

I am always challenged when I hear of someone who gave up their life of comfort to accomplish God's will for their life: like Katie Davis, who at the age of nineteen moved from Tennessee to Uganda. She settled into Jinja, a little village nestled between the Nile River and Lake Victoria, where she lives as a missionary. Katie started out teaching hundreds of children and has now adopted fourteen girls. How does a normal Christian teenager who wore cute clothes, drove a yellow convertible, and dated a hot guy end up in Jinja with fourteen adopted daughters? She is not a super-spiritual Christian; like most of us she loves God but she also enjoyed the conveniences of life.

She enjoyed her life in America: she was homecoming queen, president of her high school class, and looking forward to attending college. In her autobiography, *Kisses from Katie*, she says, "The fact that I loved Jesus was beginning to interfere with the plans I once had for my life

> To live a life that's worthy of the sacrifice you are making in surrender may require you to be brave, maybe even a bit reckless.

and certainly the plans others had for me.... Slowly but surely I began to realize the truth. I had loved and admired and worshipped Jesus without doing what He said.... I wanted to actually *do* what Jesus said to do. So I quit my life."[1]

I love this! The life of this young woman is impacting so many lives today in Uganda and all over the world. Katie had such a deep revelation of surrender to the point of being reckless and brave. It might be dangerous to have faith for what God is calling you to, but it's even more dangerous to choose comfort over your mission.

Whenever someone asked Jesus about what being a disciple was all about, what the expectations were for following Him, He tested their willingness to surrender, to "quit their life." The rich young ruler found this out the hard way. He thought being a follower of Jesus was about keeping the rules and following the law. Jesus lovingly counters his wrong thinking with this: "One thing you lack...go, sell everything you have and give it to the poor, and you will have treasure in heaven. Then come, follow me" (Mark 10:21).

The word *then* stands out to me. We must surrender

first and *then* follow. Many times we want to follow God to be sure we can trust Him, and then surrender at a later time. Surrender first, then follow; trust first, then follow; obey first, then follow...you get the pattern.

Obviously God is not asking all of us to sell our belongings and move to Uganda, but He is asking us to be willing to serve Him no matter the cost. Surrendered ones, like Katie, love people and see potential in each life. Surrendered people are excited when they hear words such as *impossible, incurable,* or *can't.* Their lives are so dependent on God that they don't regard any obstacle as insurmountable.

It's not that surrendered people never fail; it's that they are unrelenting and refuse to give up on God. Living life surrendered is not easy, but it is simple. Each day simply seek out the God-encounters in your path, in your school, at your place of work. You may not be able to reach a child in Uganda, but you can reach one across the street. All of our stories may not be as extraordinary as Katie's, but they can be just as powerful and impactful. Surrendered people see God in the ordinary things in life.

PRACTICAL SURRENDER

It goes without saying that women are great at multitasking. We have been endowed with multilevel, intricate neuron receptors. These highly advanced, complex neurons in our left-sided brain allow us to perform multiple, sophisticated modus operandi such as apply makeup, send an e-mail, give our husbands directions on the phone, and think of yet another creative way to cook chicken for dinner, all at the same time seamlessly and easily.

All the things we juggle and cradle in the span of a day

are dizzying to try to categorize, including, but not limited to, wife, mother, daughter, sister, friend, chauffeur, chef, dry cleaner, physician, lawyer, coach, manager, administrator, and on occasion, sex goddess. This is why, when our companions of the opposite gender plop themselves on the couch at the end of the day and say something like, "I am so exhausted. We both work so hard," we think in our heads, "Oh, that's precious. You're adorable!" It's OK to take great pride in crowning ourselves the queens of multitasking, but let it not be at the expense of missing out on interruptions that are really God-encounters. Is your surrender to God showing outwardly in the sensitivity of your heart to His voice?

There are God-interruptions, potential miracles awaiting you at work, in your commute, in your class at school, at the grocery store, sitting next to you on a plane or on a bus, or sitting next to you in church. Jesus performed many miracles "on His way" somewhere. The woman with the issue of blood, Jairus's dead child, the paralyzed man, the boy with epilepsy, the woman with her alabaster box, demon-possessed children, the blind man, the lame man, the sick people, all of them were so-called interruptions. Jesus's first miracle—He was interrupted at a wedding. His second miracle—He was interrupted on the way to Galilee.

I wonder how many miracles we have missed out on simply because we weren't interruptible. How many times has our haste led us to walk by a human need and, in so doing, miss out on being a part of God's wonder-working power? The surrendered life is about more than just meeting together in our own little circles. We must see God in the ordinary things of life and meet others' needs.

BE THE CHANGE

Part of this is simply cultivating your awareness, becoming aware of social justice causes in the world. Read books that reveal the needs in your city, state, country, and the world at large. When was the last time something moved you to action, not only to prayer or tears or pity but also to act? I love the story in Acts 3 of Peter and John. One is the speaker of the house, the other the one Christ loved. They represent a divine pairing, truth tempered with love. They are at the gate called Beautiful, an ornate, magnificent structure, made of brass, located on the eastern side of the temple. It is reported that it took twenty men to close it and became a choice spot for begging so people could practice the "act" of piety before petitioning God.

On this particular day Peter and John practically had to step over the lame man just to get into the temple, and so they stopped to talk with this man. I find it interesting that they were able to connect a needy man like this on the outside with the prayers they were about to offer on the inside of the gate. So many times our surrender to God stays within the four walls of the church, but the effects of surrender should reach far beyond our church circles.

In many ways this beggar is also a picture of sinful man, paralyzed by sin, unable to enter into God's presence, needing complete, immediate, and total healing. Peter and John were able to see past his afflictions to his deepest need. Peter and John were intentional about bringing this man into their world, starting with eye contact and a loving touch. They didn't stand back and watch; they leaned in and engaged the man.

True compassion is not helpless pity; it spurs us to

action! I like the way *The Message* paraphrases this idea: "Don't push your way to the front; don't sweet-talk your way to the top. Put yourself aside, and help others get ahead. Don't be obsessed with getting your own advantage. Forget yourselves long enough to lend a helping hand" (Phil. 2:3–4). The Greek word for *compassion* has the same root as the word for *moved,* and it means to be moved inwardly, to yearn with tender mercy, affection, and empathy.[2] It can be defined as sympathy coupled with a desire to help, sharing the feelings of others and possessing a desire to help them.

Remember the story of the good Samaritan? Many passed by and ignored the needs of the man. He had been robbed, stripped, wounded, and left for dead. It's up to us, surrendered ones, to see the need and be moved with compassion to then act on their behalf. It's not

> Surrendered ones live full and die empty.

enough to be prompted by love and inspired by hope; we must also be moved to action by faith. This is precisely what made Jesus so magnetic while He walked the earth. Indifference creates callouses on our hearts while compassion creates callouses on our hands. Surrendered ones live full and die empty. Joyce Meyer says it this way: "Indifference makes excuses; love finds a way."[3]

Sometimes when we see the depth of poverty, injustice, and sin in our world, it's almost easier to ignore it than try to do something. It's easy to feel overwhelmed by the needs we see around us, but once we are aware, ignorance is no longer an option. Abraham Lincoln said, "To sin with silence, when they should protest, makes cowards of men."[4] Don't get lost in statistics; remember that behind every number is a name and a face. I read this piece by an unknown author that illustrates this perfectly:

> A man fell into a pit and couldn't get himself out.
> A philosopher came along and said, "You only think that you are in a pit."
> A news reporter wanted an exclusive story on the person in the pit.
> A realist said, "This was no accident, you know. Only bad people fall into a pit."
> A mathematician calculated how the individual fell in the pit.
> A geologist told him to appreciate the rock strata in the pit.
> A fundamentalist said, "You deserve your pit."
> A charismatic said, "Just confess that you're not in a pit."
> A philanthropist came by and said, "We brought you some food and clothing while you're in the pit."
> An IRS worker asked if he was paying taxes on the pit.
> A self-pitying person said, "You haven't seen anything until you've seen my pit."
> An optimist said, "Things could be worse."
> A pessimist said, "Things will get worse!"
> Jesus, seeing the man, took him by the hand and lifted him out of the pit.

Surrendered ones are like Jesus. They can be found in the pits of life, extending a helping hand for any who will receive it.

RECKLESS GENEROSITY

One thing that marks the lives of people who truly surrender to God is that they are generous. Generosity involves more than how much money you give away; it involves the way you live your life. Think of the early church in Acts; those believers were absolutely unstoppable. God ignited a breathtaking revolution using a handful of radical Christ-followers who were willing to give of themselves to the cause of Christ. They are the perfect picture of a surrendered, generous church. "Everyone was filled with awe, and many wonders and miraculous signs were done by the apostles. All the believers were together and had everything in common. Selling their possessions and goods, they gave to anyone as he had need" (Acts 2:44–45).

It's the idea of surrender and sacrifice to God that so deeply satisfies you that you are excited to see what God will do with what you let go of.

The result of the inward surrender of the early church was the outward sign of being generous and resulted in this: "And the Lord added to their number daily those who were being saved" (Acts 2:47). God is the same yesterday, today, and forever. He is still looking for radical followers to continue to change the world. And one thing He's looking for in those followers is generosity.

The early church excelled in this. When the Bible mentions how effective they were, how fast they grew, or how much impact they had, many times it is prefaced by how generous they were. They gave willingly and liberally, making sure that everybody's needs were met. True generosity is not just about money; it's more about your willingness to give and the condition of your heart. It's the idea of surrender and sacrifice to God that so deeply satisfies you that you are excited to see what God will do with what you let go of.

The enemy tries to tell us that if we let go of anything that belongs to us—our lives, our hearts, or our resources—we will lose it. That's the way the world thinks, that if you let go of something, you will lose it. God's kingdom does not work the same way; it's actually the opposite. Something happens in your heart when you let go of something and you are left with an open hand; that thing is called faith. Being generous builds your faith in Christ.

So many of us are so afraid of what will happen if we let go of the blessings God has given us: our lives, our resources, our hearts. We simply cannot entertain the possibility that we will be left with an open hand. We are not willing to take the risk of not getting anything back, so the tendency is to hold on to what we have. We live from this posture: closed hand and closed heart.

Surrender asks you to open your heart and your hands to God. Ironically this is the only posture and position that can receive anything from God, because God can't fill a closed hand, and God can't fill a closed heart—only an open hand and an open heart. God will not force our hands open. He simply offers us something better in return if we'll let go of what is already ours. An open hand is reflective of an open heart, and God honors both of those!

Being generous is worth the risk of letting go and sacrificing what is in your hand—your time, your money, your heart, your life—so that you can be a part of what God is doing. That is the only way to be unstoppable for the kingdom of God. More than money we've been given gifts, talents, and abilities to share with the world. The parable of the three servants who were given talents is a great illustration of this. God is the ultimate giver. The Master gave to His servants generously! He set the tone.

> He throws caution to the winds, giving to the needy in reckless abandon. His right-living, right-giving ways never run out, never wear out. This most generous God who gives seed to the farmer that becomes bread for your meals is more than extravagant with you. He gives you something you can then give away, which grows into full-formed lives, robust in God, wealthy in every way, so that you can be generous in every way, producing with us great praise to God.
> —2 CORINTHIANS 9:8–11, THE MESSAGE

The first two servants put their talents to work. They had to release their talents in order to invest them and bring back a profit from what the Master had deposited with them. God has given you divine capital: life, creativity, potential, personality, and experiences. What are you doing with these talents? Are you actively investing like the first two servants, or are you playing it safe like the third servant? "But the man who had received the one talent went off, dug a hole in the ground and hid his master's money" (Matt. 25:18).

The third servant played it safe and achieved nothing with what was given to him. If we choose not to live generous, surrendered lives, this is what we will become, as well. This is the tragedy of unused potential. The reality is that if our goal is to live a risk-free Christian life, avoiding pain at all costs, avoiding sacrifice and inconvenience because we're afraid to trust God, we end up bringing more pain on ourselves than if we just choose to let go and trust God.

Generosity requires you to defy and overcome fear. The third servant also let fear take root in his heart, and he was unwilling to take the risk of doing something with what he was given. "Then the man who had received the one talent came.... 'So I was afraid and went out and hid your talent in the ground. See, here is what belongs to you'" (Matt. 25:24–25). Do you realize you can tithe faithfully without ever being a generous giver *if* your heart is full of fear rather than faith when you give? The wicked servant returned what already belonged to the master and nothing else, because his heart was full of fear. This is what we do when we give the first 10 percent of all that we make to God: we return what belongs to Him.

Think about your life. When you give of your time, resources, money, and life, are you playing it safe, or are you allowing your faith to overcome your fears? Remember, we too, like the third servant, will have to face God one day to settle accounts about what we did with what we had. My prayer for you is that you would surrender yourself so unreservedly to God that you would urgently plead for the privilege of giving. "But just as you excel in everything— in faith, in speech, in knowledge, in complete earnestness and in your love for us—see that you also excel in this grace of giving" (2 Cor. 8:7).

I want to live the kind of generous life that appreciates the goodness of God in my life. For some reason the third servant in the parable says this: "Master...I knew that you are a hard man, harvesting where you have not sown and gathering where you have not scattered seed" (Matt. 25:24). This strikes me as odd because he was talking about the same master as the first two, but he saw the master in a very different light. I wonder why the third servant had such a different experience with the master. Perhaps the difference was in *how* he received his talents. Maybe the fact that he only received one talent played into why he hid it, maybe he was resentful of the others who had more, or maybe he felt like he should have been given more.

There are times in our lives when we fail to see the opportunity in what God has given us because we are so focused on what others have. No matter what you have been given, whether little or much, trust that God in His fairness gives according to our ability.

Surrendered ones live the kind of life that does not struggle to receive what God has given them. Honestly the reason some of us struggle to surrender to God is because we have a hard time receiving God's free gift of love and acceptance. I have talked with people who approach God with a little bit of suspicion and are skeptical.

I remember watching *Oprah* one afternoon. It happened to be one of her "favorite things" episodes, in which she gives away expensive gifts to every member of the audience. If you have ever watched any of these shows, then you know that the crowd goes absolutely berserk when they realize they are about to get thousands of dollars of *free* merchandise from Oprah! As soon as she mentions what show it is, the surprised audience members erupt in animated excitement; people begin to cry tears of joy, jump up and down like schoolchildren, and even run around the studio in excitement.

The show started, and Oprah began rolling out cart after cart of electronics, fashion accessories, jewelry, and then at the very end...a car! My mouth dropped open;

every single lucky audience member was getting keys to a brand-new car. I was shocked by her generosity, but then, in the back of my mind, I was a little bit suspicious. Why was she *really* doing this? Maybe she was getting a tax break for donating the cars? Or maybe it was a public relations gimmick to increase her popularity? There *must* be something in it for her.

Maybe Oprah did have ulterior motives, because we are all flawed human beings. But the problem is, we bring that same attitude when we approach God's generosity to us. Apart from an authentic, real relationship with God, you cannot comprehend true generosity. Even after we give our lives to Christ, we need to continually renew our minds to overcome cynicism, suspicion, and doubt so we can successfully receive from God.

"Freely you have received, freely give" (Matt. 10:8). This is the language of the message of salvation; this is the message of the gospel and the surrendered Christian life. You can't freely give if you have not freely received, and you can't freely receive if you don't freely give. Two servants received a gift that changed their lives, while one did not even allow the gift to touch his life because he did not receive it in the right spirit.

You can't give generously if you don't know how to receive generously. God wants us to receive from Him generously. "For you know the grace of our Lord Jesus Christ, that though He was rich, yet for your sakes He became poor, that you through His poverty might become rich" (2 Cor. 8:9, NKJV).

Jesus became poor by giving up His rights as God to become human. He surrendered His glory and His rights for you and me in an act of reckless generosity. He is asking us to do the same. There are things we need to give recklessly to those around us to spread the love of Jesus. What can you be recklessly generous with today? Don't let fear cause you to hide your talent for love and your willingness to give in the ground. Playing it safe and taking the path of least resistance will not yield a big harvest. Releasing what God has placed in your hands and in your life will. As you receive God's love, it will motivate you to surrender completely to Him. The result of this is a wide-open, generous life that touches those around you and brings God glory.

Chapter Twelve

BLESSED ASSURANCE

God is in the slums, in the cardboard boxes where the poor play house. God is in the silence of a mother who has infected her child with a virus that will end both their lives. God is in the cries heard under the rubble of war. God is in the debris of wasted opportunity and lives, and God is with us if we are with them.[1]

—BONO

ONE SUNNY FLORIDA afternoon as I drove home from church, I stopped at a red light at a familiar intersection. I drive past that same stoplight each time I go to church. Today, though, I saw an unfamiliar sight. It was a woman sitting, with her feet tucked under her skirt, by the cement culvert close to the grass. She was young, probably in her early twenties, and she had a square sign with barely legible scribbling on cardboard appealing for help. Her straggly strands of auburn hair dangled in her face, while tattered, stained clothing hung loosely on her thin frame.

The first time I saw her out of the corner of my eye, I tried to do anything but achieve any eye contact with her. I changed the channel on my radio, looked at my text messages, and readjusted my seat belt. I even cleaned up the trash I left in the side compartment of my air-conditioned, leather-upholstered vehicle. I didn't want to look straight at her because I knew that once I looked her full in the face and allowed her big, brown eyes to meet mine, I would have to do something. I felt bad for her; it was a hot Florida day, and I had no idea how long she had already been sitting in the sun. But I was already running late for a lunch date with a friend and I had a busy day of errands ahead of me before heading back to church for the evening service.

Just think about that for a minute; I had *just* left church and yet could not *be* the church when an opportunity presented itself. It was a long red light, and I grew more and more uncomfortable with each passing minute. I managed another sidelong glance at her and noticed she had no shoes on and her feet were scarred and filthy. Dirt caked the outside of them and settled deep into the crevices on her heels. Looking at her disheveled appearance made me feel bad, but not bad enough to do something about it. I have been on many missions trips to Peru, Guatemala, and Zimbabwe where I saw people who live in abject poverty that I don't have the words to describe. For some reason we are more comfortable with poverty on the shores of a distant land than at the intersection down the street from our church.

God Needs Us to *Be* the Church

Inward surrender *must* have an outward working. How are you leaving an impact on the people around you? Many of us have an encounter with Jesus, He changes our lives, and then we go on to live happily ever after. We never get out of our comfort zone in service to others. We still have a consumer mentality in our relationship with God; we go to church hoping the band sings our favorite worship songs; we want to be entertained by the message and then leave in time to make it for lunch at the restaurant.

God did not save you so you can sit on your blessedness! He saved you and asks you to get up from the comfort of your life and rescue those who are dying without Him. Surrendered people do not just experience the Christian life so they can bask in it; they have an urgency to serve this God who has so ravished their lives. I eventually turned my car around that sunny Florida day, stopped by a restaurant to buy some food, and drove back to that same intersection. She was still there, holding her cardboard sign on the side of the road. I had to make a U-turn so she would be on the driver's side of my car. I rolled down my window, asked her if she was hungry, and then gave her the hot, healthy meal I had bought. Does what I did make me a saint? No. It was me simply being a Christian.

If we truly have experienced the joy of salvation, then there should be a *tangible* change in our lives. There was a prophet who had this kind of experience. The prophet Isaiah in Isaiah chapter 6 and verses 1–8 had an astounding

Inward surrender must have an outward working.

vision of the presence of the almighty, transcendent, majestic God! He did not just see a king; he saw the King of kings seated in His majesty, His glory literally filling the temple.

Even the holy angels are humbled in His presence, covering their faces because they can't look upon the face of a holy God. They are flying and their feet can't even touch the ground because the ground is holy ground. Their only job for all of eternity is to cry out, "Holy, holy, holy is the LORD Almighty" (v. 3).

Isaiah encounters the presence of God and hears the question, "Whom shall I send? And who will go for us?" (v. 8). He sees the need to consecrate himself afresh to God. He can barely speak, but he is able to verbalize this sentiment: "Here am I. Send me!" (v. 9). I have heard so many excuses from people when given an opportunity to serve, to give, or to step out in faith for God.

They say things such as the following:

- I'm really busy. I work two jobs, and I'm just trying to make ends meet. When things settle down, I will be able to serve.

- The economy is really bad right now, my savings took a big hit in the down economy, and my nest egg is fried and scrambled.

- I'm afraid of what will happen if I go on a missions trip. What if something bad happens?

- I'm too old to do anything for God now. I've already lived my life. It's time for the young ones to take over.

- I'm too young to serve God. When I'm done with college or married with kids, then I'll do something for God.

Isaiah gave no excuses, no alibis, no reasons for his inactivity. Isaiah simply surrendered himself fully and completely with reckless abandon on the altar of commitment. When God is asking you to give more than you think you can, instead of refusing, why not ask Him for the faith and grace to do it? The last thing God wants is for us to encounter His presence just so we can bask in it. He is not asking us to get so filled up with Him that we are spiritually obese. We have such access to the Word of God—on our phones, in our homes, on blogs, podcasts, and books—that it's easy to take in more than we're giving out. If you were to count how many Bibles you have access to, both written and electronically, I'm sure it would surprise you.

LIFT, TRIM, AND TUCK

Spiritual obesity is a problem in the church today. If you are always asking who is going to meet your needs and not asking whose needs you can meet, you might be obese. If you're taking in more spiritual calories than you're giving out, without looking for ways to exercise your spiritual muscles, chances are you have some spiritual "jiggly bits." Jiggly bits are the parts of you that are still moving when the rest of you is no longer in motion. Oh, yes, the dissection of the anatomy of a jiggly bit is so necessary.

Others of us may have a myriad of symptoms of spiritual obesity: bloated muffin tops, puffy back fat, an overflowing uniboob, a stomach bulge, and let's not forget bat wings. Bat wings are muscles that had every intention of being a tricep but at the last minute decided to fall flat and baggy. Chances are, your grandma has them. You'll know for sure if she does because they almost slap you in the face when she's pointing at something.

On a serious note, some of us don't need more Bible study, or more teaching, more twelve-step programs, or more empowerment videos. All those things are great and helpful, but if we are constantly taking in more and more truth and knowledge without giving an outlet of service and exercising our spiritual muscles, we have a problem!

The Message version of Hebrews 12:1–3 says it this way:

> Do you see what this means—all these pioneers who blazed the way, all these veterans cheering us on? It means we'd better get on with it. Strip down, start running—and never quit! *No extra spiritual fat,* no parasitic sins. Keep your eyes on Jesus, who both began and finished this race we're in. Study how he did it. Because he never lost sight of where he was headed—that exhilarating finish in and with God—he could put up with anything along the way: Cross, shame, whatever. And now

he's there, in the place of honor, right alongside God. When you find yourselves flagging in your faith, go over that story again, item by item, that long litany of hostility he plowed through. That will shoot adrenaline into your souls!

—EMPHASIS ADDED

That passage makes me feel like I can go out and conquer the world!

I have a deep, profound revelation for you today; are you ready for it? Serving is like spiritual Spanx. God bless Sara Blakely, who invented Spanx while watching the *Oprah* show, as Oprah was complaining about the annoyance of tears and runs in pantyhose. If you don't know what Spanx are, first of all, you're in the minority and the rest of us secretly don't like you. I'm just slightly kidding. Spanx is a full-body undergarment with girdle-like qualities that flatter your figure. They really do make you look streamlined in clothes, and we love the way we look in them, but just like any other girdle, it is hard work to get them on and even harder work to go the bathroom with them on. Did I mention they are full bodywear?

This begs the question, why do we put ourselves through such anguish? We do it because the end result is always worth the effort. Spanx, like serving, trims you down, shapes you up, controls all your jiggly bits, and forces you to take on a particular shape. It's time to trim down our excess spiritual fat, exercise our spiritual muscles, and get fit. The great thing about serving is that it doesn't artificially make you look good on the outside like Spanx— it literally transforms you from the inside out.

AND NOW WHAT?

Remember my story from the beginning of the book? On the road to healing from the tragedies I faced, there was a point at which I said, "All right, God, I surrender; now what?" Maybe you have asked that question at least once in your life; maybe you are asking yourself that right now. The answer to the *now what* question is to open your eyes to the needs of those around you and find a place where you can be the solution to a problem.

I have a friend who became aware of the horrendous worldwide phenomenon of human slave trafficking. Human trafficking recently became the second most profitable criminal industry in the world, surpassing weapons trafficking. It is modern slavery and is a heinous crime. One day as my friend was going for her morning run, she was praying and pleading with God to show her what she could do about it. She says God asked her what she was doing right now. She replied and told God that she was running, and an idea was born. Every year hundreds participate in a run to raise funds for an organization dedicated to fighting human trafficking. Thousands of dollars have been raised to date, dollars that translate into saved lives.

> The answer to the *now what* question is to open your eyes to the needs of those around you and find a place where you can be the solution to a problem.

That money represents young girls being rescued, hearing the gospel of Jesus, having a new lease on life and hope! My friend did not have to go out and create anything; she just used what she was already doing to make a difference. God is not asking you to go out and reinvent the wheel. Find out what organizations in your community are fighting for a cause you are passionate about and then join them. You don't have to be rich or gifted to be used by God; you just have to be willing.

God wants you to take on a certain shape. Not only does serving change your shape, but when you serve, you also start to take on His shape. You become more like Him, more like God. Matthew 20:28 tells us, "Just as the Son of Man did not come to be served, but to serve, and to give his life as a ransom for many." Each of us can bring something unique and special when we serve because God has given us certain things that make us uniquely shaped for service. Rick Warren talks about this in *The Purpose-Driven Life*.[2]

Your SHAPE includes the following:

- Spiritual gifts

- Heart (another word for that is passion)—
  When was the last time something moved
  you to action, not only to tears or pity but
  also to act? Where is that holy discon-
  tent with injustice in the world? Ask God
  to open your eyes and stir up your passion.
  We were created to be passionate people, to
  be passionate about bringing freedom and
  light to the dark places of your world. Have
  the courage to look at suffering and not
  be overwhelmed. Let this encourage you
  always: "The Spirit of the Sovereign LORD
  is on me, *because* the LORD has anointed
  me to preach good news to the poor. He
  has sent me to bind up the brokenhearted,

to proclaim freedom for the captives and release from darkness for the prisoners" (Isa. 61:1, emphasis added).

- Abilities—What are you good at? What do you excel at? What things add strength to you and fuel you to dig deeper, go further, and invest greater?

- Personality—God wants to use you and your zany self for His glory. You don't have to change who you are for God to use you; He wants you just the way you are.

- Experience—Everything has been given to you by God to shape you, to equip you, and to empower you to serve. Don't hide your painful past, but allow God to heal you and then turn around and share that with others. God sometimes surrounds you with people who need to hear your past so it won't become their future.

Our surrender is for the purpose of serving our world and becoming rivers of living water, rather than stagnant cesspools. The Bible tells us the sober truth that each of us shall give account of ourselves to God. We are supposed to be like a flowing river of water, not a retention pond. A good way to assess this is to ask yourself, "If everyone at my church served the way I serve, gave the way I give, and is as committed as I am, what would our church look like?"

Dear friend, don't wait one more day. If you aren't serving, then you're just existing. God is calling us to a higher level through surrender. Get off your blessed assurance and go serve your world.

IMPRINT YOUR WORLD

Bill Bright, the founder of Campus Crusade for Christ (or Cru in the United States) and one of the great Christian leaders of the twentieth century, was once asked why God has used Him so mightily. Through his ministries, Campus Crusade for Christ, the *Four Spiritual Laws* tract, and the *Jesus* film, more than one hundred fifty million people have come to Christ and will spend eternity in heaven. His reply was that when he was a young man, he made a contract with God; he literally wrote it out and signed his name at the bottom.

It said, "From this day forward, I am a slave of Jesus Christ."[3] Would you be willing to sign such a contract in your heart? Do you have a heart for God and His house? Are you surrendered to God? Make a decision today

> Get off your blessed assurance and go serve your world!

to give it all to God: your past, your regrets, your present problems, your future ambitions, your fears, dreams, weaknesses, habits, hurts, and issues.

Declare in the presence of the living God today, "I can trust God, I need God, I will worship God with my life, and I will surrender." What will it look like for you to surrender fully to God? I don't know. It will look a little different for each person. It means that each day you have to offer yourself afresh and seek God's will. Say, "Not my will, but Yours be done," or in other words, "As You wish." God's will for you is different in some respects from His will for me. There's no formula I can give you other than urging you to simply offer your life—all that you are and all that you do—every day to God. "As You wish."

PRAYER WORKS

The best way for me to honor the life of my wonderful mother is to surrender my life totally, completely, and unconditionally to God. By walking out my God-given purpose, I continue her destiny. Beyond that, by the grace of God, I will pass it on to my children. My pen will now become a baton to those who come after me. When my voice is one day no more, my words will still speak through these pages. I hope no one has to go through what I went through before I came to my place of surrender, but sometimes that is what it takes to become who God created you to be.

There is a certain place you will reach when you live for God. It is a place that tests your surrender and forces you to decide, once and for all, whether you trust the God you love. I had a happy, little comfortable Christian life with no major bumps in the road or struggles. One day, suddenly, everything was turned on its head. I was blindsided by the harshness of the reality that things don't always work out for Christians. Just because I serve God is not a guarantee for a life devoid of heartache and disappointment. Yes, I am aware that God works all things out for our good, but honestly not all things that happen to us are good. My experience forced me to mature as a believer and to find out if I really loved this God that I served.

Perhaps you have been through such an experience. Mine was a journey that lifted me through the peaks and heights of expectation and then plunged me to the depths of desperation. In between the heights and the depths there were highlands of self-discovery and inspiration. The woman I am today is a result of the girl who discovered that God is greater than my understanding and His love for me is deeper than my imagination. This same God will do the same for you.

> *Dear Lord, would You lead us to a place of true surrender? Help us to embrace the life You have for us by losing ourselves in You. We declare by the authority we have as children of the most high God that we will trust You, we do need You, we will worship You with our lives, and we will surrender. In Jesus's most holy and precious name we pray, amen.*

SMALL GROUP STUDY GUIDE

CHAPTER ONE: WHOSE LIFE IS IT ANYWAY?

Talk it out

When you hear the words "as You wish," what comes to mind and why?

How do love and surrender intersect? What relationship do the two share?

Think about your life. Is there anything that you desire more than God?

What do you think about the following statement: "Our surrender to God has just as much to do with our bodies as anything else." Why?

Walk it out

Surrender is not passive or automatic, but it is powerful and requires human action. We need to understand that the reason surrender is so integral to our relationship with God is because it helps us relate to God.

- The next time you study your Bible, meditate on Romans 12:1–2 and Galatians 2:20.

- How can we have the same attitude that Jesus had when it comes to surrendering to God?

If you struggle in any area of your physical body, make a decision now to give that struggle to God and create an action plan for your unique situation.

- Set three or more practical, measurable goals.

- Find one or two friends who will keep you accountable and inform them of your goals.

CHAPTER TWO: BATTLE OF WILLS

Talk it out

Have you fully surrendered your life to Jesus Christ? There are only two possible answers: yes or no.

Walk it out

If your answer is no, then the very next thing you must do is to wave your white flag of surrender in the battle of living life your way or God's way.

- Being a good person does not make you a Christian; giving your life to Jesus does.

- Right now, in your heart, say a prayer asking God to be your Lord and Savior. Tell Him you receive the free gift of salvation and want to be a follower of Jesus Christ all the days of your life.

- If you pray this with sincerity and believe in your heart that Jesus is your Lord, you have started the best relationship on earth, and a lifetime of adventure awaits you!

If your answer is yes, then you must ask yourself, "Is my surrender full and complete?"

- Are you an unsurrendered Christian? One who has the Holy Spirit within them but still preferring to live life on your own terms?

    1. Identify the one or two areas where you have refused to let God direct and control your life.

    2. Develop an action plan of what practical steps you will take in the next seven days to allow God to infiltrate every part of your life and heart.

    3. Be specific. Write down how to give those areas over to God and who will keep you accountable.

    4. Using the Bible as a guide, pray explicitly over those areas of your life and be expectant to see change.

CHAPTER THREE: QUEEN OF HEARTS

Talk it out

To what or whom are you yielding your heart?

What or who is defining your identity right now? If God removed you from your current position at work or school, would you feel empty and unfulfilled?

In what ways might you be holding on to people and things for security that only God should give you?

Walk it out

Do a heart check right now and follow the checklist below, asking yourself these questions and writing down your answers in a journal.

- Am I willingly giving over my heart to God? If not, what areas do I need to surrender to Him?

- Am I overcommitting and doing too much? Do I regularly feel tired and overworked?

- Am I leaving enough room in my schedule for rest, leisure, and downtime?

After you have written down your answers, look to find any major patterns or glaring red flags in the assessment of your heart.

Devote some time to prayer for those areas, and listen to hear what the Holy Spirit speaks to your heart.

CHAPTER FOUR: THE FEAR FACTOR

Talk it out

All fear is rooted in lies that we believe about ourselves that operate as distractions for our minds. How is fear distracting you from what God may be asking you to do or give up for Him?

Distractions steal our ability to love God with all our minds. What tricks do fear and distractions play on your mind?

Fear can also pollute our minds. Read Philippians 4:8–9. How does this verse apply to fear? What is the end result in verse 9 of applying what verse 8 tells us to do?

What kinds of things do you spend your time thinking about? Why?

How can you renew your mind with the Word of God. What can help combat the mind games?

What price are you willing to pay to truly be fearless? What would living fearlessly look like for you?

Walk it out

Read James 1:23–25 and pray that God would show you a picture of your heart. Ask Him to reveal the areas where you need to rid yourself of fear and distractions.

- Name your biggest fear or distraction that is keeping you from loving God with *all* your mind and heart.

- Fill in the blank in this sentence: I will erase _____ from my mind and replace it with _____.

CHAPTER FIVE: ALMOST DOESN'T COUNT

Talk it out

How would you honestly categorize yourself—as an "almost Christian" or as a fully devoted disciple? Why would you describe yourself this way?

What is the number-one obstacle you face when you consider going "all in" for God and surrendering to Him completely?

How you make decisions is a good reflection of whether your heart is surrendered to God. What or who is your motivating factor in decision making? What does the Bible have to say about this?

Walk it out

Rate yourself on a scale of one to five on the following statements,. one being a definite NO and five being a definite YES.

- Are you fully devoted to God in your faith?

- Have you surrendered completely in the area of finances: tithing consistently and even giving above the tithe?

- Do you love God with all your heart? Is there any area that is off limits to Him?

Get more specific. Define what areas of your life are off limits to God?

What is stopping you from handing that part of your life over to God completely?

CHAPTER SIX: PIG THEOLOGY

Talk it out

Think about the following statement: "Self-sacrifice through self-control is necessary for self-fulfillment." How does this reflect the heart behind surrender? Does this accurately represent *your* beliefs about surrender?

What sacrifices do you need to make to go from being involved with the things of God to being truly committed?

Part of being committed is being willing to endure suffering in order to see what you are passionate about actually take place.

- What are you passionate about?

- What do you believe God has gifted you to do? Is there a way your passion and your talents can combine and be used to serve others?

- What price are you willing to pay to see your destiny come to pass?

Walk it out

God has a unique calling on all of our lives. Prayerfully ask God to show you what you are gifted and created to do—if you don't already know. Then write these statements down in a journal, filling in the blanks.

- I am created to _____.

- I can make a difference in my world by

  _____.

- I believe the impact I was born to make is to

  _____.

- The Spirit of God inside me has empowered me to

  _____.

Read Isaiah 61:1–3 and then prayerfully fill in this blank. "The Spirit of the Lord is upon me and has anointed me to _____

_____

_____."

CHAPTER SEVEN: SURRENDERED YET POWERFUL

Talk it out

If the idea of surrender intimidates you or causes you to withdraw, what is the source of this feeling? Do you have negative past experiences with surrender that you are pulling from?

When was the last time you turned the mirror inward and performed a heart check, really examining the nooks and crannies of your inner person? Be honest with yourself and ask the tough questions. Why don't you want to submit your will to your spouse, boss, or parent?

What script is playing in your head and mind when you resist submitting your will to someone else?

Meditate on Philippians 2:5–11. How can the mind that was in Christ Jesus also be in you? What was the link between Christ's surrender to God and His authority in heaven and on earth? What is the link between surrender to God and your strength as an individual?

Walk it out

Intimacy with God is the foundation of our authority in Christ and the key to walking in power. It all starts with the knowledge of who God is as revealed in His Word.

- Do you have a regular, daily, consistent time of prayer and Bible study? If not, this is where you should start.

- Make an action plan on how to increase your intimacy with God over the next seven days.

- Keep a journal and record what God reveals to you during your time of prayer and study.

- Use the SOAP method for Bible study.[1]

    S for Scripture—As you read the Bible, be on the lookout for verses that relate to you or really stick with you after you have finished reading. You can highlight them in your Bible.
    O for observation—Once you have identified the verses that really speak to you, ask God to reveal Himself to you through His Word. Now is a good time to start writing down in your journal ideas as they come to you.

A for application—How is this verse relevant to your everyday life? What practical thing(s) can you extract from the passage and start using in your life right away? Does this passage challenge you? Are you inspired by what you have read?

P for prayer—This is an important stage in creating intimacy with God. Be honest in your prayer time, and tell God what is on your heart. Then listen to what He has to say.

CHAPTER EIGHT: GLORIOUS RUINS

Talk it out

What kind of expectations do you place on the following people in your life?

- Your spouse

- Your family members

- Your friends

- God

When people do not meet your expectations of them, what is usually your first response? Why?

Read Hebrews 12:3, compare your situation to Christ, weigh your offense against what Jesus endured. How does that change the way you view things?

Walk it out

The idea of surrendering to God is offensive to some people because of past negative experiences with abuse of spiritual authority, or a simple lack of trust in God.

203

- Think back over your life and your past experiences with surrender and submission. Do you have any offense toward God or others?

- What negative experiences turned you off from desiring to submit yourself to another person? Ask God to help you release the past right now.

- Write down the top one or two areas in which you do not trust God and pray specifically for those areas.

Finally, start the process of forgiving those who may have offended you in the past. Let it go and let God begin to heal you.

CHAPTER NINE: LOSING CONTROL

Talk it out

How do you feel when you're not in control of a situation that will have an impact on your life?

Have you ever had to act on something God told you to do even though you did not agree with it? How did you handle the situation?

Do you believe that God is telling a story with your life? If so, how does this affect how you react when things don't go the way you think they should? In what ways can you show God you trust Him as you wait for Him to come through for you or answer a prayer?

Walk it out

Read Luke 9:23–24. How can you practically apply this to your life?

What does it look like for you to daily deny yourself and follow Jesus?

- How does this affect your daily schedule?

- In what way does this affect how you budget your money?

- What effect does this have on your relationship with others?

CHAPTER TEN: LOOK BOTH WAYS

Talk it out

What do you think about the following statement: "From the example of the past, the man of the present acts prudently so as not to imperil the future"?

What lessons can you learn from your past that will help you as you look to the future?

What does the phrase "acts prudently" mean to you?

What kind of legacy are you leaving right now? What are you building with your life through your daily actions and desires for the future?

How are you living with the future in mind? What does this look like in your life?

Let us not hold the blessings of God so tightly that we are not willing to let them go if He asks us to. We have to hold on to God tighter than we hold on to the blessings God gives us. Is your surrender complete and unreserved, or are you holding something back? Why?

Walk it out

First, write down the biggest lie you have believed about surrender that has stopped you from completely and unreservedly giving all of yourself to God.

Next, write out a truth from God's Word that counters that lie.

Finally, write down a declaration of faith. Describe how you will apply that truth to your life from now on. For example:

- I used to think that if I surrendered to God then,

    _____.

- I now recognize that as a lie and know that the Word of God tells me that _____.

- In faith, I declare that I will _____.

CHAPTER ELEVEN: BOLD AND RECKLESS

Talk it out

Study Matthew 28:18–20. How does the Great Commission work itself out in your life practically? What do you believe is your mission in life?

What are you living for? Does this line up with what you believe God is calling you to do?

What are you living for? If money were no object, what would you love to do with your life and your talents?

What do you exist for? When you wake up each day, what do you live to do?

How is your surrender to God showing outwardly in the sensitivity of your heart to His voice?

Walk it out

Write down a few ways that you are leaving an impact on the people around you.

Challenge yourself. Pray about a way you can leave your comfort zone in service to others. Consider the following avenues:

- Get involved in serving at your local church.

- Pray about going on a missions trip.

- Try to read at least one book this year that deals with a social justice cause. Some suggested readings would include *Half the Sky* by Nicholas Kristof, *Undaunted* by Christine Caine, and *Kisses From Katie* by Katie Davis.

CHAPTER TWELVE:
BLESSED ASSURANCE

Talk it out

Can you identify a tangible difference that surrender to God has made in your life? A change that you can see and observe? What is that difference?

How does your surrender to God affect the way you serve the world around you? What is your motivation for reaching out beyond the four walls of the church to reach the world for Jesus?

In what practical ways do you see the need to serve your neighbor, your community, your city, and your country?

Walk it out

What do you know for sure to be true about surrender in your life and what that looks like for you? Study the Word of God with this in mind for the next few days. Increase your knowledge of what the Bible has to say about surrender.

Next, apply that knowledge to your life. What does it mean for you, personally, to surrender yourself to God completely and without reservation?

Next, simply surrender yourself to God; in prayer and in deed.

Finally, obey what God tells you to do next, no matter how it makes you feel.

Evaluate your SHAPE: Identify at least one of these attributes in your life and describe how you can use that in service to others.

- Study Romans 12:6-8. What spiritual gifts do you have? If you are unsure, pray for God to reveal this to you, and take note of where you tend to function in your local church.

- Heart: What are you passionate about? What kinds of things cause you to not just to feel bad but also to be moved to act in compassion?

- Abilities: What are you good at? What do you excel at? What things add strength to you and fuel you to dig deeper, go further, and invest greater?

- Personality: What makes you uniquely you? List two or three personal characteristics that make you stand out from others. How might God use those things in service to others?

- Experience: What things have you endured in your past that could help another person? Think of all the things you have been through, then identify one or two that could encourage another person. Write these down in a journal.

NOTES

Chapter One: Whose Life Is It Anyway?

1. William Goldman, *The Princess Bride* (Orlando, FL: Harcourt Books, 2003).
2. *The Princess Bride*, directed by Bob Reiner (Los Angeles: 20th Century Fox, 1987), DVD.
3. Elisabeth Elliot, *Shadow of the Almighty: The Life & Testament of Jim Elliot* (New York: Harper & Brothers, 1958), 19.
4. Adapted from Warren Wiersbe, *The Bible Exposition Commentary*, 2 vols. (Wheaton, IL: Victor Books, Scripture Press, 1989), 530.
5. A. W. Tozer, *The Pursuit of God: The Human Thirst for The Divine* (Camp Hill, PA: WingSpread Publishers, 2006), 23.
6. Frederick Bruce, *The Letter of Paul to the Romans: An Introduction and Commentary* (Leicester, England: InterVarsity Press, and Grand Rapids: Wm. B. Eerdmans Publishing Co., 1985), 213.
7. Blue Letter Bible. "Dictionary and Word Search for *logikos* (Strong's 3050)," http://www.blueletter bible.org/lang/lexicon/lexicon.cfm?strongs=G3050 (accessed June 4, 2013).

Chapter Two: Battle of Wills

1. Goodreads.com, "C. S. Lewis Quotes," http://www .goodreads.com/quotes/110054-the-more-we-let-god -take-us-over-the-more (accessed June 5, 2013).

2. Goodreads.com, "Elisabeth Elliot Quotes," http://www.goodreads.com/author/quotes/6264.Elisabeth_Elliot (accessed June 5, 2013).
3. A. W. Tozer, *The Divine Conquest* (N.p.: Revell, 1950).

CHAPTER THREE: QUEEN OF HEARTS

1. Brainyquote.com, http://www.brainyquote.com/quotes/quotes/a/anaisnin120256.html (accessed June 5, 2013).
2. Christine Caine, *Can I Have It and Do It All, Please?* (Sydney, Australia: Equip & Empower Ministries, 2009).
3. Philip Hughes, *Paul's Second Epistle to the Corinthians* (London: Marshall, Morgan & Scott, 1962), 453. Viewed online at Google Books.
4. James Strong, *The New Strong's Exhaustive Concordance of the Bible* (Nashville, TN, Thomas Nelson Publishers, 1990), s.v. *"charis,"* G5485.
5. Ibid., s.v. *"arkeo,"* G714.
6. Ibid., s.v. *"dunamis,"* G1411.
7. Ibid., s.v., *"teleiotes,"* G5047.
8. Ibid., s.v., *"teleo,"* G5055.
9. Ibid., s.v. *"astheneia,"* G769.
10. Bill Johnson, *When Heaven Invades Earth* (Shippensburg, PA: Destiny Image Publishers, Inc., 2003).

CHAPTER FOUR: THE FEAR FACTOR

1. Goodreads.com, "Oswald Chambers Quotes," http://www.goodreads.com/author/quotes/41469.Oswald_Chambers (accessed June 5, 2013).

2. Rick Warren, Twitter, April 19, 2013, https://twitter
.com/RickWarren/status/325118182283173888
(accessed June 11, 2013).

3. Lisa Bevere, *Girls With Swords* (Colorado Springs,
Colorado: WaterBrook Press, 2013), 7.

CHAPTER FIVE: ALMOST DOESN'T COUNT

1. "I Surrender All" by Judson W. Van DeVenter. Public
domain.

2. Rick Warren, *The Purpose-Driven Life* (Grand
Rapids, MI: Zondervan, 2002), 233.

CHAPTER SIX: PIG THEOLOGY

1. Rhonda H. Kelly, *Divine Discipline* (Gretna, LA: Pel-
ican Publishing Company, 1992).

2. As related in Zig Ziglar, *Embrace the Struggle:
Living Life on Life's Terms* (New York: Howard
Books, 2009), 79.

3. Strong, *The New Strong's Exhaustive Concordance of
the Bible*, s.v. "*pascho*," G3958.

CHAPTER SEVEN: SURRENDERED YET POWERFUL

1. Brennan Manning, *The Importance of Being Foolish*
(New York: HarperCollins Publishers, 2005).

2. "Turn Your Eyes Upon Jesus" by Helen H. Lemmel.
Public domain.

3. Johnson, *When Heaven Invades Earth*, 99–100.

Chapter Eight: Glorious Ruins

1. Goodreads.com, "Oswald Chambers Quotes," http://www.goodreads.com/quotes/561300-all-god-s-revelations-are-sealed-to-us-until-they-are (accessed June 6, 2013).
2. Joyce Meyer, *The Love Revolution* (New York: Faith-Words, 2009), 195.
3. *Merriam-Webster's Collegiate Dictionary*, 10th Edition (Springfield, MA: Merriam-Webster, Inc., 1999), s.v. "thrive."

Chapter Nine: Losing Control

1. Arthur Bennett, ed., *The Valley of Vision: A Collection of Puritan Prayers and Devotions* (Carlisle, PA.: The Banner of Truth Trust, 1975), 91.
2. Jeff Goins, "When Life Doesn't Turn Out the Way You Expect," http://storylineblog.com/2012/09/26/when-life-doesnt-turn-out-the-way-you-expect/ (accessed June 6, 2013).
3. John Eldredge, *Epic: The Story God Is Telling* (Nashville: Thomas Nelson, 2004).

Chapter Ten: Look Both Ways

1. As quoted in Os Guiness, *God in the Dark* (Wheaton, IL: Crossway Book, 1996).
2. Marianne Williamson, *A Return to Love* (New York: HarperCollins Publishers, 2009).
3. Tim LaHaye, *How to Win Over Depression* (Grand Rapids, MI: Zondervan, 1974).

CHAPTER ELEVEN: BOLD AND RECKLESS

1. Katie Davis, *Kisses From Katie* (New York: Howard Books, 2011).
2. Strong, *The New Strong's Exhaustive Concordance of the Bible*, s.v. *"splagchnizomai,"* G4697.
3. Meyer, *The Love Revolution*.
4. Brainyquote.com, http://www.brainyquote.com/quotes/quotes/a/abrahamlin135434.html (accessed June 6, 2013).

CHAPTER TWELVE: BLESSED ASSURANCE

1. Goodreads.com, "Bono Quotes," http://www.goodreads.com/quotes/385905-god-is-in-the-slums-in-the-cardboard-boxes-where (accessed June 7, 2013).
2. Warren, *The Purpose-Driven Life*.
3. Rick Warren, "Bill Bright: Quiet Giant of 20th Century," *Orlando Sentinel*, July 30, 2003, http://articles.orlandosentinel.com/2003-07-30/news/0307300191_1_bill-bright-crusade-for-christ-campus-crusade (accessed June 7, 2013).

SMALL GROUP STUDY GUIDE

1. Adapted from Stovall Weems, *Awakening: A New Approach to Faith and Fasting and Spiritual Freedom* (Colorado Springs, CO: WaterBrook Press, 2010), 131–132.

PASSIO

PASSIONATE. AUTHENTIC. MISSIONAL.

Passio brings you books, e-books, and other media from
innovative voices on topics from missional living to
A DEEPER RELATIONSHIP WITH GOD.

Visit the Passio website for additional products and
TO SIGN UP FOR OUR FREE NEWSLETTER

www.PASSIOFAITH.com

www.twitter.com/passiofaith | www.facebook.com/passiofaith

PASSIO
THE ART OF AUTHENTIC FAITH

12002